Food Security

M. M. Eboch, Book Editor

Published in 2022 by Greenhaven Publishing, LLC
353 3rd Avenue, Suite 255, New York, NY 10010

Copyright © 2022 by Greenhaven Publishing, LLC

First Edition

All rights reserved. No part of this book may be reproduced in any form without permission in writing from the publisher, except by a reviewer.

Articles in Greenhaven Publishing anthologies are often edited for length to meet page requirements. In addition, original titles of these works are changed to clearly present the main thesis and to explicitly indicate the author's opinion. Every effort is made to ensure that Greenhaven Publishing accurately reflects the original intent of the authors. Every effort has been made to trace the owners of the copyrighted material.

Library of Congress Cataloging-in-Publication Data

Names: Eboch, M. M., editor.
Title: Food security / M. M. Eboch, editor.
Description: First edition. | New York : Greenhaven Publishing, 2022. | Series: Introducing issues with opposing viewpoints | Includes bibliographical references and index. | Audience: Ages 12–15 | Audience: Grades 7–9 | Summary: "Anthology of diverse viewpoints that address food insecurity in the United States. Includes volume introduction, color photos, critical thinking material, resource material."— Provided by publisher.
Identifiers: LCCN 2020050040 | ISBN 9781534508019 (library binding) | ISBN 9781534508002 (paperback)
Subjects: LCSH: Food security—United States—Juvenile literature.
Classification: LCC HD9000.5 .F596435 2022 | DDC 363.80973—dc23
LC record available at https://lccn.loc.gov/2020050040

Manufactured in the United States of America

Website: http://greenhavenpublishing.com

Contents

Foreword 5
Introduction 7

Chapter 1: Who Suffers from Food Insecurity?
1. There Is a Difference Between Food Insecurity and Hunger 11
   Food Forward
2. Food Insecurity Is Worldwide 17
   Fondazione Barilla Center for Food & Nutrition
3. College Students Go Hungry, Too 21
   Denise-Marie Ordway
4. Many Seniors Cannot Afford Adequate Food 29
   Center on Budget and Policy Priorities
5. Food Insecurity Is Linked to Major Chronic Diseases 35
   Susan Perry

Chapter 2: What Causes Food Insecurity?
1. We Must Curb Population Growth 41
   Population Connection
2. Don't Blame Population Growth 47
   Joe Hasell
3. Tackle Climate Change to Improve Food Security 55
   Concern Worldwide US
4. College Students Need More Help 61
   Emily Moon
5. Food Deserts Are Connected to Poor Health and Food Insecurity 67
   Food Empowerment Project

Chapter 3: How Can We Ensure That People Have Food Security?
1. Technology Can Meet the Demand 77
   Ashley Hunter
2. Genetically Modified Food Can Eliminate World Hunger 82
   Jennifer Ackerman
3. Food Security Is Land Security 89
   Michael Igoe Devex

4. Eat Plants, Not Animals *Dana Ellis Hunnes*	97
5. Let's Eat Insects *Rick LeBlanc*	102
Facts About Food Security	108
Organizations to Contact	111
For Further Reading	114
Index	117
Picture Credits	120

Foreword

Indulging in a wide spectrum of ideas, beliefs, and perspectives is a critical cornerstone of democracy. After all, it is often debates over differences of opinion, such as whether to legalize abortion, how to treat prisoners, or when to enact the death penalty, that shape our society and drive it forward. Such diversity of thought is frequently regarded as the hallmark of a healthy and civilized culture. As the Reverend Clifford Schutjer of the First Congregational Church in Mansfield, Ohio, declared in a 2001 sermon, "Surrounding oneself with only like-minded people, restricting what we listen to or read only to what we find agreeable is irresponsible. Refusing to entertain doubts once we make up our minds is a subtle but deadly form of arrogance." With this advice in mind, Introducing Issues with Opposing Viewpoints books aim to open readers' minds to the critically divergent views that comprise our world's most important debates.

Introducing Issues with Opposing Viewpoints simplifies for students the enormous and often overwhelming mass of material now available via print and electronic media. Collected in every volume is an array of opinions that captures the essence of a particular controversy or topic. Introducing Issues with Opposing Viewpoints books embody the spirit of nineteenth-century journalist Charles A. Dana's axiom: "Fight for your opinions, but do not believe that they contain the whole truth, or the only truth." Absorbing such contrasting opinions teaches students to analyze the strength of an argument and compare it to its opposition. From this process readers can inform and strengthen their own opinions, or be exposed to new information that will change their minds. Introducing Issues with Opposing Viewpoints is a mosaic of different voices. The authors are statesmen, pundits, academics, journalists, corporations, and ordinary people who have felt compelled to share their experiences and ideas in a public forum. Their words have been collected from newspapers, journals, books, speeches, interviews, and the internet, the fastest growing body of opinionated material in the world.

Introducing Issues with Opposing Viewpoints shares many of the well-known features of its critically acclaimed parent series, Opposing

Viewpoints. The articles allow readers to absorb and compare divergent perspectives. Active reading questions preface each viewpoint, requiring the student to approach the material thoughtfully and carefully. Photographs, charts, and graphs supplement each article. A thorough introduction provides readers with crucial background on an issue. An annotated bibliography points the reader toward articles, books, and websites that contain additional information on the topic. An appendix of organizations to contact contains a wide variety of charities, nonprofit organizations, political groups, and private enterprises that each hold a position on the issue at hand. Finally, a comprehensive index allows readers to locate content quickly and efficiently.

Introducing Issues with Opposing Viewpoints is also significantly different from Opposing Viewpoints. As the series title implies, its presentation will help introduce students to the concept of opposing viewpoints and learn to use this material to aid in critical writing and debate. The series' four-color, accessible format makes the books attractive and inviting to readers of all levels. In addition, each viewpoint has been carefully edited to maximize a reader's understanding of the content. Short but thorough viewpoints capture the essence of an argument. A substantial, thought-provoking essay question placed at the end of each viewpoint asks the student to further investigate the issues raised in the viewpoint, compare and contrast two authors' arguments, or consider how one might go about forming an opinion on the topic at hand. Each viewpoint contains sidebars that include at-a-glance information and handy statistics. A Facts About section located in the back of the book further supplies students with relevant facts and figures.

Following in the tradition of the Opposing Viewpoints series, Greenhaven Publishing continues to provide readers with invaluable exposure to the controversial issues that shape our world. As John Stuart Mill once wrote: "The only way in which a human being can make some approach to knowing the whole of a subject is by hearing what can be said about it by persons of every variety of opinion and studying all modes in which it can be looked at by every character of mind. No wise man ever acquired his wisdom in any mode but this." It is to this principle that Introducing Issues with Opposing Viewpoints books are dedicated.

Introduction

"Biotechnology is no panacea for world hunger, but it's a vital tool in a toolbox, one that includes soil and water conservation, pest management, and other methods of sustainable agriculture, as well as new technologies."
—Channapatna Prakash, agricultural scientist

We all know what hunger feels like. It might start as a vague desire for food. Then the stomach starts to growl. Left unchecked, the empty stomach cramps painfully with demands to be filled. Most people don't let hunger get that far. But hundreds of millions of people around the world—including millions in the United States—have no choice. They regularly don't get enough to eat.

Even people who don't suffer from constant hunger may suffer from food insecurity. Someone may have enough food to survive but may live in constant worry over how to pay for the next week's groceries. They may have to choose between paying for food, housing, medicine, or their children's school fees. They may depend on food pantries or school lunch programs. In some households, parents go hungry so that children can eat.

According to the US Department of Agriculture, over 11% of the total US population lived in food-insecure households in 2018. Those rates skyrocketed as the COVID-19 pandemic put millions out of work. Although the data for people who lived with food insecurity in 2020 is not yet available, some food banks reported a 70% increase in demand.

Food insecurity is higher among seniors and among households that contain children, especially those households led by single mothers. But no age group is exempt. Millions of college students report challenges getting enough to eat. Hispanic households have twice the rate of food insecurity as white households. Black households have an even higher rate, with more than one in five experiencing food insecurity.

Everyone can agree that hunger and food insecurity are problems that should be solved. That's where the agreements stop.

What causes food insecurity? Some say population growth is the biggest problem, as the world population heads toward 9 billion. Others point to climate change causing more droughts and flooding that destroy cropland. Land ownership also presents challenges, especially in developing countries. Big agricultural businesses put small farmers out of work. The big businesses might produce more food more quickly, but that doesn't help the farmers who have lost their land. In some cases, the extra food production goes to feed livestock. The meat is then sold to the rich, while the poor stay hungry.

Do we even need more food? We currently have the ability to grow enough food for everyone. However, one-third of the food produced is never consumed. In low- and middle-income countries, the bulk of this loss is destroyed by pests, mold, or other spoilage before the food gets to the markets. In high-income countries such as the United States, a similar percentage of food is thrown out after it is purchased. Either it spoils before use, or people prepare too much and throw away the extra. If we ended this wastefulness, would we end hunger?

Getting food to the people who need it is another problem. Not everyone has access to grocery stores, especially in poor urban areas. There, people may depend on convenience stores that offer a limited selection at higher prices. High prices mean some people can't afford the food that is available. In particular, a healthy diet that includes high-quality fruits and vegetables may be too expensive or unavailable.

Limited food choices, whether because of lack of access or high prices, can cause people to suffer from health issues that seem contradictory. Those who shop mainly at convenience stores and fast food restaurants have higher rates of obesity and its associated health problems, such as diabetes and heart disease. At the same time, they may suffer nutritional deficiencies due to a diet based on junk food rather than healthy options. The health issues cause higher medical bills, leaving even less money for healthy food.

With many factors in play causing food insecurity, debate also rages over how to solve the problems. Do we need land reform, to keep more land in the hands of small farmers? Can technology solve the problem, by producing more food with the same land or by eliminating wasted food? Maybe genetically modified foods are the answer. They can be modified to tolerate heat and drought, to resist diseases, or to be toxic to pests. However, these foods have been available for only a few decades, with new ones hitting the market every year. Their eventual effect on the environment and human health is uncertain.

Perhaps the answer lies in our eating habits. Should everyone go vegetarian or vegan? Meat production takes more land and water then plant production. On the other hand, livestock can eat food waste scraps and graze land that isn't suitable for crops. Maybe the answer lies in eating more meat—in the form of insects, which provide a nutritious, high-protein diet that doesn't demand as much from the environment.

The questions around food security lead to many possible answers. The current debates are explored by authors of the diverse viewpoints contained in *Opposing Viewpoints: Food Security*, shedding light on this ongoing contemporary issue.

Chapter 1

Who Suffers from Food Insecurity?

Many communities maintain food refrigerators, which offer free food to anyone who needs it.

There Is a Difference Between Food Insecurity and Hunger

"We could say that hunger is one potential consequence of food insecurity, but food insecurity does not always result in hunger."

Food Forward

In the following viewpoint, authors from Food Forward cover the basics of food insecurity versus food security. Food security is not merely about having enough food. The food should also be healthy and taste good. It should also be culturally appropriate. This means the people buying or receiving the food are familiar with it, know how to prepare it, and can read any labels or instructions. Food Forward is an organization that rescues thousands of pounds of surplus produce each week and donates it to hunger relief agencies across Southern California.

"What Is Food Insecurity? Food Security?" Food Forward, Inc, October 18, 2017. Reprinted by permission.

AS YOU READ, CONSIDER THE FOLLOWING QUESTIONS:
1. What is food insecurity?
2. What is the difference between hunger and food insecurity?
3. Why does this relief organization want to understand different levels of food security?

Since we talk about food security and food insecurity quite a bit here at Food Forward, we thought it would be helpful to define both terms, what they mean, and how we measure them. Here's our definition:

food insecurity refers to a lack of access to enough good, healthy, and culturally appropriate food.

There's a lot going on there, so let's unpack it a bit.

Enough: this one's the easiest. Everyone needs to eat, and we all need to eat a certain amount to stay healthy, active, and happy.

Good: this is where things get a bit hairy (or pear-y). Good is a relative word. What's good food for you might not be good food to your friend, sibling, neighbor, or co-worker. But instead of ignoring the vagueness of this term, we should embrace it! Everybody deserves to eat food that they think is good, right? Nobody should have to eat peas if they hate peas but love carrots (Mom & Dad, are you reading this?).

Healthy: we love healthy food here! Healthy food is nutritious and sustaining. It's full of vitamins, minerals, fiber, energy, and all the other things that our bodies need to be happy.

Culturally appropriate: like "good," this term brings us back into the subjective realm. Having access to culturally appropriate food means that people have food that they are familiar and comfortable with. It's knowing how to shop for it or select it, prepare and cook it, and how to enjoy it! Part of this is availability of familiar foods and varieties, but it also could include things like the language of the label and instructions.

Many Americans take food security for granted. For some families, enjoying nutritious and abundant meals is a luxury.

What Is Food Security?

The definition of food security is, as you might imagine, just the opposite! Food security means having reliable access to enough good, healthy, and culturally appropriate food. It means that you or your family aren't worried about paying for groceries, where your next meal might come from, or cutting back on food in order to pay the bills.

Food security is related to all sorts of other great and wonderful ideals like food justice, food sovereignty, and food equity. While food security is certainly a crucial part of these, concepts such as food justice and food sovereignty tend to have broader social, economic, and cultural implications. So food security is an important part of food justice, but not the whole of it.

What's the Difference Between Food Insecurity and Hunger?

While food security and hunger are related, they are not the same. In fact, the USDA recently removed references to hunger in their food security measurements (https://www.ers.usda.gov/topics/food-nutrition-assistance/food-security-in-the-us/measurement/), citing the need for a separate and more detailed study on hunger. Here are some key differences between the two:

First, food security is socio-economic (financial and cultural), while hunger is physiological (physical). Studies on food security attempt to measure reliable access to food, with questions that include anxiety over shopping, budgeting for healthy meals, and running out of food. Hunger, on the other hand, is a physical sensation. We could say that hunger is one potential consequence of food insecurity, but food insecurity does not always result in hunger.

Second, we measure food security at the household level and hunger at the individual level. A family experiencing food insecurity may have some members that go hungry and others who do not. For example, parents in food insecure families might have enough food to feed their children, but might experience hunger themselves.

How Do We Measure Food Insecurity?

So, with all this talk about what it is, how do we actually measure something like food insecurity. Food Forward and most other hunger-relief nonprofits rely on measurements that the USDA conducts annually. Every year tens of thousands of households respond to their short survey (https://www.ers.usda.gov/topics/food-nutrition-assistance/food-security-in-the-us/measurement/#measurement), which is added onto the census.

There are only 10 questions, and an additional 8 questions for families with children. The questions ask about various indicators of food insecurity, ranging from the least severe ("We worried whether our food would run out before we got money to buy more") to the most severe ("In the last 12 months did you or other adults in your household ever not eat for a whole day because there wasn't enough money for food").

Once the answers are collected, the USDA groups households into the 4 classifications of food security: high food security, marginal food security, low food security, and very low food security. Households are considered to have low food security if they reported experiencing 3 or more indicators of food insecurity. Households are considered to have very low food security if they reported 3 indicators of food insecurity AND some degree of eating less than they should/skipping meals.

> **FAST FACT**
> According to the US Department of Agriculture, 37.2 million people lived in food-insecure households in 2018. That's over 11% of the total population.

Keeping It Simple

This system of measuring food security allows families to self-report their own experiences, and also keeps the results very clear. It gives us a very simple measurement to look at: what percent of households reported 3 or more indicators of food insecurity. This keeps things easy for those of us who care—individuals, volunteers, policy makers, students, you and me—to understand.

But despite how simple it may seem, the study is actually quite complex! Years and years of research have gone into defining and refining the questions and analysis of results. While some people might think that the simplicity of the method leads to less reliable results, in fact that's not the case at all (if you don't believe me, you can read this 130 page statistical analysis and report! https://www.ers.usda.gov/webdocs/publications/47603/34533_tb-1936.pdf?v=41274). The study keeps our understanding of food security and food insecurity clear and accurate.

Why Talk About Food Security at All?

Food security and food insecurity are really important concepts for us to think and talk about. By moving the discussion of food policy beyond hunger (which again, refers only to a physical sensation), food insecurity captures the reality of individuals and families who struggle to get enough food.

Finally, these terms give us a working definition and standard for measurement. This allows community organizers, non-profit leaders, policy makers, and government officials to talk with each other and work together to create plans that will improve overall access to food, health, and wellness. Because even as we dive into definitions, studies, and statistics, the overall goal is to secure everyone's right to eat well and be well.

EVALUATING THE AUTHOR'S ARGUMENTS:

Viewpoint author Food Forward explores ways of looking at food security and insecurity. Do you agree that it is important to understand different ways a person or family might have food insecurity? How would this knowledge affect the way the problem might be addressed?

Viewpoint 2

Food Insecurity Is Worldwide

Fondazione Barilla Center for Food & Nutrition

In the following viewpoint, the Fondazione Barilla Center for Food & Nutrition looks at food insecurity worldwide. While many people may assume food insecurity is an issue for developing countries, in fact it is more widespread. People may struggle with food security even in developed countries, such as the United States and countries in the European Union. In addition, even when people have enough food, they may suffer from nutritional deficiencies. The author argues that the nutritional quality of people's diets should be considered with any national food security program. The Barilla Center for Food & Nutrition Foundation (BCFN) explores food related issues and works for healthier and more sustainable lifestyles.

"Who said that there are no problems in the so-called developed countries in finding enough food?"

AS YOU READ, CONSIDER THE FOLLOWING QUESTIONS:
1. How is food insecurity linked to hospital visits?
2. Why is the quality of food in a diet important?
3. How have worldwide hunger rates changed in recent decades?

"Food Insecurity: Not Just a Problem for Developing Countries," Fondazione Barilla Center for Food & Nutrition, July 22, 2016. Reprinted by permission.

Who said that there are no problems in the so-called developed countries in finding enough food? As set out in detail in the latest edition of *Eating Planet*, there are many factors which currently threaten food security, defined by the United States Department of Agriculture (USDA) as "access by all people at all times to enough food for an active, healthy life," on a global level and not just in the poorest countries.

The Categories Most at Risk

The clearest example of this situation undoubtedly comes from the USA, where despite the general state of well-being, there is a significant number of people suffering from different types of malnutrition. This is also shown by a study recently published by the journal *Population Health Management*, demonstrating that over half of the patients in the study who were frequently admitted to hospital—more than 3 times over the previous year—did not have regular access to healthy food and even didn't always have enough food in the house. The reasons which lead to these seemingly extreme circumstances are actually very common: those who suffer most from food insecurity are elderly people, people on low incomes or those who have difficulties going out to buy food and cook it or who are dependent on others (relatives, institutions or charities). Nevertheless, the results of this study are not entirely surprising given that back in 2014, according to data from USDA, around 15% of families in the USA claimed they had problems accessing food.

> **FAST FACT**
>
> In 2018, an estimated 821.6 million people did not have enough to eat, according to the WHO. Hunger is most common in Africa, while the largest number of undernourished people (more than 500 million) live in Asia.

People in Europe Eat More, but Not Better

The situation in Europe is not radically different. The General Overview of Food Insecurity 2015 focusing on Europe and Asia and published by experts from the FAO—the UN organisation in charge of food and

A child at an Afghan refugee camp holds out her plate asking for food. Malnutrition and undernourishment are problems in Europe and Central Asia.

agriculture—highlights the fact that in Europe and Central Asia, food insecurity has gradually evolved from being a problem of insufficient calories, to one of food quality, which is more subtle and difficult to identify. According to the data in the report, Eurasia achieved the goal of halving the incidences of hunger by 2015, reducing the number of undernourished people to under 5%. However, another problem remains, that of malnutrition, which affects the rich and poor countries in the region to a similar extent. Indeed, there has been an increase in the number of people suffering from micronutrient deficiencies with dangerous health consequences as well as those who are overweight or obese. "Both these conditions are common, even among children under 5 and may well have a major impact on the economies of these countries," explain the FAO experts. They suggest that a better national food security programme should be designed, and that "not enough focus is given to the quality of people's diets."

Who Suffers from Food Insecurity?   19

Climate Change and Economic Policies Are Making It Harder for People to Access Food

Access to food is not simply a question of land productivity or personal income. Various sections of *Eating Planet* focus on the effects of climate change on productivity and the availability of food, but this on its own does not explain why the situation is so serious, even for the richest countries. Indeed, there are a range of other factors which need to be considered, such as the economic crisis which has altered families' buying power and the balance of the markets. In some cases, this has led to dangerous speculation on prices, or conflicts in strategic areas of food production, which also create problem for the countries in those areas attempting to import their food provisions. However, some progress has been made in the field of food security. According to the FAO in the State of Food Insecurity in the World 2015, the number of people suffering from hunger has fallen to 795 million (216 million less compared to the period 1990/1992), but there is still much more work to be done.

EVALUATING THE AUTHOR'S ARGUMENTS:

The viewpoint author states that food insecurity and malnutrition are problems worldwide. At the same time, obesity and associated health concerns are also problems. What does the author suggest about access to food and the importance of healthy food?

Viewpoint 3

College Students Go Hungry, Too

Denise-Marie Ordway

"Nearly 1 in 3 traditional-age students from low-income families are cutting or skipping meals, eating less than they should and going without food."

In the following viewpoint, Denise-Marie Ordway explores the problem of food insecurity among college students in the United States. Colleges and universities are beginning to recognize that many of their students may not get enough food to eat. Food insecurity can cause physical and mental health problems and lower a student's grade point average. Some institutions are responding by offering free or low-cost groceries to students. Researchers also recommend making it easier for college students to receive government benefits such as food stamps in order to address food insecurity. Denise-Marie Ordway is a journalist who has worked for newspapers and radio stations in the US and Central America.

"College Student Hunger: How Access to Food Can Impact Grades, Mental Health," by Denise-Marie Ordway, Journalist's Resource, March 30, 2019. https://journalistsresource.org/studies/society/education/college-student-hunger-food-pantry/. Licensed under CC BY-ND 4.0.

AS YOU READ, CONSIDER THE FOLLOWING QUESTIONS:
1. How can food insecurity affect college students' grades?
2. What other negative effects can result if a college student doesn't get enough healthy food?
3. How are race and childhood poverty connected to college students who don't get enough food?

Just a few years ago, the College and University Food Bank Alliance, which helps schools establish food pantries, had 184 members. By early 2019, though, the number had more than tripled to 700-plus members.

As tuition rises and the other costs of college go up, campus administrators are forced to face a troubling reality: Many college students don't get enough to eat. In response, hundreds of schools—from community colleges to Ivy League universities—have opened food pantries or stores selling subsidized groceries. Many students ages 18 to 49 are not eligible for the federal government's Supplemental Nutrition Assistance Program, also known as food stamps.

At Cornell University, the student-run Anabel's Grocery attracted about 2,000 unique customers within the first several months, according to the student newspaper. The store offers "low-cost groceries for all Cornell students and subsidies for those who qualify." At the Knights Helping Knights Pantry at the University of Central Florida, students can pick up five free food items a day. Portland Community College opened pantries on all four of its campuses and created a co-op with free school supplies, bus passes, clothes and other items.

Academic research shows that a substantial percentage of college students experience "food insecurity," a lack of access to adequate amounts of food, especially healthy foods. The proportion appears to vary by institution type and among student groups, with racial and ethnic minorities being most likely to skip meals or go hungry. The research also suggests students who don't have enough food are more likely to have low grades and poor health.

Below is a sampling of academic research on these subjects.

"College Students and SNAP: The New Face of Food Insecurity in the United States"

From the City University of New York's Graduate School of Public Health and Health Policy and Temple University's College of Education, published in the *American Journal of Public Health*, December 2019. By Nicholas Freudenberg, Sara Goldrick-Rab and Janet Poppendieck.

College students are a new group at risk for food insecurity—a problem explained by five trends, according to this analysis of academic studies, news media reports and three researchers' experiences studying and addressing food insecurity at multiple universities.

The five trends:
- A higher proportion of college students are from households with incomes at or below the poverty line than were in the past.
- College is more expensive now than in the past.
- The purchasing power of the Pell grant, a federal grant for lower-income students, has fallen over time.
- It's tougher to pay for college while working. "Coupled with rising college prices, students must work nearly full-time to afford full-time community college," write the authors. "To avoid paying for benefits, today's employers, including universities, often divide fulltime hours across multiple parttime workers, contributing to the growing number of students working several jobs to make ends meet."
- Higher education institutions have less money to spend on student support programs. State funding, the authors write, "has decreased by 25% per student over the last 30 years, and states have cut $9 billion from higher education in the last 10 years alone. In public universities, budget cuts have led to significant reductions in student services."

The researchers find that a number of individual colleges try to help students get food by introducing a range of programs, including food pantries, subsidized cafeteria meals and emergency loans and grants. However, the researchers recommend that the government and schools work to boost the number of college students who participate in the federal Supplemental Nutritional Assistance Program, commonly referred to as SNAP or food stamps. "Because food pantries are often the first point of contact between food-insecure students and university resources, they can become hubs for screening and enrolling eligible students in SNAP and other public benefits, publicizing affordable meals on campus, and engaging students in organizing for food justice as well as distributing food," the authors write.

"Hunger in Higher Education: Experiences and Correlates of Food Insecurity Among Wisconsin Undergraduates from Low-Income Families"

From the University of Iowa and University of California, San Diego, published in *Social Sciences*, September 2018. By Katharine M. Broton, Kari E. Weaver and Minhtuyen Mai.

This study finds that the college students who are most likely to report experiencing the lowest levels of food security are racial and ethnic minorities and those who live off campus, attend college in urban areas and grew up in homes without reliable supplies of food.

The three researchers analyzed data from a longitudinal study of 3,000 low-income, undergraduate students who attended 42 public colleges and universities in Wisconsin in 2008. They also conducted in-depth interviews with a random sample of 50 of those students approximately every six months between 2008 and 2010 and then each year through 2012. In late 2009, almost 1,400 of the individuals studied answered another round of questions about their experiences buying and finding adequate food.

Some other key takeaways: "Among a sample of traditional-age students from low-income families, we found that nearly 1 in 3 are cutting or skipping meals, eating less than they should and going without food due to limited resources. All of the students received financial aid and most worked and received support from family, but they still struggled to get enough to eat. Students identified a lack of money and time—rather than a lack of knowledge regarding cooking or budgeting—as major barriers to their food security."

A surprising number of college students in the United States do not have enough to eat.

"Experiences with 'Acute' Food Insecurity Among College Students"

From San Diego State University, published in the *Educational Researcher*, January 2018. By J. Luke Wood and Frank Harris III.

This study looks at which groups of college students are most likely to experience food insecurity. The analysis, based on survey data from 6,103 students in southern California, found that multiethnic and black students were most likely to say they have "challenges with hunger"—an acute form of food insecurity. Sixteen percent of black students and 16.5 percent of multiethnic students reported going hungry compared to 10.4 percent of Latino students and 9.2 percent of white and Asian students. The study suggests some students who lack food may also lack stable housing or struggle with transportation and health issues. Colleges with food pantries "may also consider having additional services such as bus passes, free health resources, and job boards," the authors write.

"Going Without: An Exploration of Food and Housing Insecurity Among Undergraduates"

From the University of Iowa and Temple University, published in the *Educational Researcher*, December 2017. By Katharine M. Broton and Sara Goldrick-Rab.

This study looks at data on food insecurity taken from surveys representing the experiences of more than 30,000 students attending 121 colleges and universities in 26 states. More than half of undergraduates reported food-access problems. Between 11 percent and 38 percent of students enrolled in community colleges reported "very low" levels of food security, characterized by disrupted eating patterns and reduced food intake. Half of community college students also reported living in unstable housing situations.

"Efforts to increase college completion rates must be broadened to include attention to material hardship and shed light on this all-too-often hidden cost of college attendance," the authors wrote. "Stereotypes of undergraduates eating ramen noodles or couch surfing work against this."

"The Prevalence of Food Insecurity and Its Association with Health and Academic Outcomes Among College Freshmen"

From the University of Florida and nine other universities, published in *Advances in Nutrition*, 2017. By Aseel El Zein, et al.

This is another study focusing on food insecurity among college freshmen, who generally are learning to live independently after a lifetime of depending on parents and other family members. Almost 900 students from eight US colleges participated, 19 percent of whom were classified as food insecure. The researchers found that students who did not have access to adequate food "showed significantly higher perceived stress and

> **FAST FACT**
> Between 11% and 38% of students enrolled in community colleges reported "very low" levels of food security in one study. Black, multiethnic, and Latinx students are more likely to report challenges with hunger.

disordered eating behaviors and lower sleep quality." These students also were more likely to have grade-point averages below a 3.0.

"Student Hunger on Campus: Food Insecurity Among College Students and Implications for Academic Institutions"

From University of Maryland School of Public Health and University of Maryland Dining Services, published in the *American Journal of Health Promotion*, July 2017. By Devon C. Payne-Sturges, Allison Tjaden, Kimberly M. Caldeira, Kathryn B. Vincent and Amelia M. Arria.

This study found that 15 percent of undergraduates surveyed at a public university in the mid-Atlantic reported food insecurity and that another 16 percent were at risk. The researchers found evidence that students who either experienced food insecurity or were at risk were "more likely to report their overall health as fair, poor, or very poor and reported lower energy levels compared with food secure students. Food insecure students however reported more frequent depression symptoms (little interest, feeling down, feeling tired, poor appetite, and feeling bad about oneself) and that they experienced disruptions in academic work as a result of depression symptoms." Students reporting problems accessing food were more likely to live off campus and receive financial aid.

"Factors Related to the High Rates of Food Insecurity Among Diverse, Urban College Freshmen"

From Arizona State University and the University of Minnesota, published in the *Journal of the Academy of Nutrition and Dietetics*, 2016. By Meg Bruening, Stephanie Brennhofer, Irene van Woerden, Michael Todd and Melissa Laska.

This paper suggests that a high proportion of college freshmen living in dorms at one of the nation's largest public universities do not have adequate food and are more likely to report health problems such as anxiety and depression. Of the 209 freshman who participated in the study, 32 percent reported food insecurity in the previous month and 37 percent reported it in the previous three months.

"Students who rarely consumed breakfast, students who rarely ate home-cooked meals, and students with higher levels of depression were significantly more likely to report food insecurity in the past three months," the authors wrote.

"Food Insecurity Among Community College Students: Prevalence and Association with Grade Point Average"

From American University and Morgan State University, published in the *Community College Journal of Research and Practice*, 2015. By Maya E. Maroto, Anastasia Snelling and Henry Linck.

This food-access study involves students at an urban community college and a suburban community college. Sixty percent of study participants from the urban community college reported lacking adequate food compared to 53 percent of study participants at the suburban community college. Black, Hispanic and Asian students were more likely to have food-access problems than white students. Meanwhile, students battling food insecurity were much more likely to have lower grade-point averages.

> **EVALUATING THE AUTHOR'S ARGUMENTS:**
>
> Viewpoint author Denise-Marie Ordway explores food insecurity at colleges and universities. What factors seem most important in determining who suffers from food insecurity on campuses? What responses seem most appropriate?

Viewpoint 4

Many Seniors Cannot Afford Adequate Food

Center on Budget and Policy Priorities

In the following viewpoint, the Center on Budget and Policy Priorities addresses food insecurity among seniors (people age 60 and older) in the United States. The author argues that the SNAP program, commonly known as food stamps, can help seniors pay for food. That lets them save other income for expenses such as housing and health care. The rate of seniors receiving these benefits is increasing, but many are still left behind. The elderly population in the US is growing, so demand for help with food is also likely to grow. The Center on Budget and Policy Priorities studies the impact of federal and state government budget policies.

"Compared to other adult age groups, seniors are particularly vulnerable to the health consequences of food insecurity."

AS YOU READ, CONSIDER THE FOLLOWING QUESTIONS:
1. Do seniors most often live alone or with family members?
2. Are seniors the group most impacted by food insecurity?
3. What physical and mental health issues resulting from food insecurity are similar between seniors and the college students described in the previous viewpoint?

"SNAP Helps Millions of Low-Income Seniors," Center on Budget and Policy Priorities (http://www.cbpp.org), April 26, 2017. Reprinted by permission.

Nearly 67 million people in the United States are age 60 and older, and are eligible for a number of government programs designed to assist with basic life needs. Despite their eligibility for these benefits, about 6.3 million seniors, or 9 percent of seniors, live below the poverty level.[1] (See Figure 1.) Many live on fixed incomes and have limited financial means to afford expenses such as food, medical, or housing costs. Many are also disabled or take care of children. For these seniors, the Supplemental Nutrition Assistance Program (SNAP) plays an important role. While it provides a modest benefit, it enables them to shift their resources towards other immediate needs.

- SNAP provides 4.8 million seniors with resources to afford an adequate diet.[2] This represents 11 percent of all SNAP recipients in 2015.[3]
- Seniors receiving SNAP benefits mostly live alone: only 1 in 4 live in households with other members.[4]
- SNAP provided an estimated $6.6 billion to SNAP households with seniors in 2016, two-thirds of which went to households in which seniors lived alone.

SNAP Supplements Low-Income Seniors' Income

- Together, housing, health care, transportation, and food comprise the largest share of all US households' expenses.[5] SNAP helps low-income seniors—many of whom are on fixed incomes—afford food while also covering their other household expenses.

- In 2015, a typical SNAP household with an elderly member included a single elderly individual and had a monthly income of about $912 (not including SNAP), or about $10,940 a year. This income falls under the poverty line for a single-person household ($11,770 in 2015). Some 71 percent of SNAP households with an elderly member had incomes below the poverty line in 2015.

- On average, SNAP households with an elderly member received $128 in benefits each month in 2015, or about $1,500 a year, boosting their income by 14 percent.

Figure 1. Percentage of US Seniors Who Live in Poverty, 2015

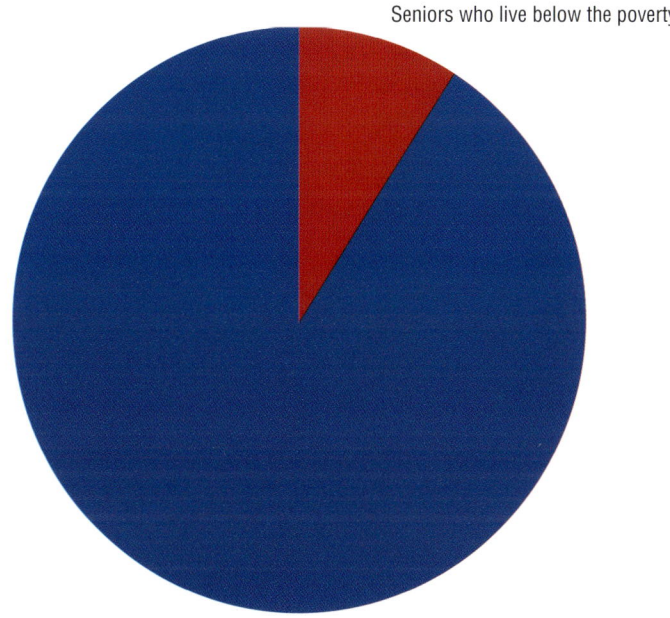

Source: US Census Bureau, Current Population Survey

Many Low-Income Households with Seniors Cannot Afford Adequate Food

- In 2015, 28 percent of all US households included individuals aged 65 and older. Of this group, 8.3 percent (2.9 million) were food insecure, meaning that these households had difficulty affording nutritious, adequate food. This share remains higher than it was before the recession, in 2007, when 6.5 percent (1.8 million) of these households were food insecure.[6]

- Food insecurity rates are higher for low-income households: in 2015, 1 in 4 US households (4.7 million) with incomes below 130 percent of the poverty line included elderly individuals. Of this group, 25 percent (1.2 million) were food insecure. Seniors lived alone in almost half (574,000) of the low-income, food-insecure households with an elderly member.[7]

- Research indicates that food-insecure seniors have less nutritious diets, have worse health outcomes, and are at higher risk for

America's senior population has grown considerably, increasing the need for government programs that address food insecurity.

depression than food-secure seniors. Compared to other adult age groups, seniors are particularly vulnerable to the health consequences of food insecurity. Households with grandchildren are almost three times as likely to be food insecure.[8] SNAP benefits help to alleviate these adverse conditions.

The Number of Low-Income Seniors Receiving SNAP Is Likely to Grow

- The number of senior SNAP recipients is likely to increase, as the elderly population, the number of seniors in poverty, and the number of seniors participating in SNAP continue to grow.
- The US population aged 60 and older has increased from 52 million to 67 million, a 29 percent increase between 2007 and 2015.[9] Over the same period, the number of seniors living below the poverty grew by 27 percent, from 5 to 6.3 million.[10]

The number of people 60 and over is projected to increase to 82 million by 2025.[11]

> **FAST FACT**
> Without Social Security, an additional 21.7 million Americans would be poor, according to the Center on Budget and Policy Priorities.

- As states have improved their outreach to seniors, the share of eligible seniors that receive SNAP has grown from 33 percent in 2010 to 42 percent in 2014. But there's still room for SNAP to improve in reaching seniors—among all individuals eligible for SNAP, some 83 percent participated in 2014.[12]

- Senior participation in SNAP is also likely to increase as food-insecure middle-aged individuals age over the coming decades and become eligible for benefits. A study of food insecurity among middle-aged individuals found that increases in food insecurity were most pronounced for people aged 40-49 and 50-59.[13] The number of individuals between 45 and 64 years old that lived below the income poverty level in 2015 was double that of the population 65 years and older.[14]

- Many of these seniors may need a lot of help. In 2015, 2 percent of the US elderly population (about a million seniors) lived with and were financially responsible for the welfare of their grandchildren. Some 31 percent of the US elderly civilian non-institutionalized population (19 million seniors) were disabled.[15]

End Notes

1. Census Bureau, 2016 Current Population Survey's Annual Social and Economic Supplement.

2. Seniors are defined as individuals aged 60 years and older, unless otherwise noted.

3. Kelsey Farson Gray, Sarah Fisher, and Sarah Lauffer, "Characteristics of Supplemental Nutrition Assistance Program Households: Fiscal Year 2015," prepared for the Food and Nutrition Service, USDA, November 2016, https://www.fns.usda.gov/snap/characteristics-supplemental-nutrition-assistance-households-fiscal-year-2015.

4. Ibid.

5. Bureau of Labor Statistics, "Consumer Expenditures in 2014," Department of Labor, October 2016, https://www.bls.gov/opub/reports/consumer-expenditures/2014/home.htm.

6. Alisha Coleman-Jensen et al., "Household Food Security in the United States in 2015," Economic Research Service, USDA, September 2016, https://www.ers.usda.gov/publications/pub-details/?pubid=79760. Seniors are defined in this report as individuals aged 65 years and older.

7. Alisha Coleman-Jensen et al., "Statistical Supplement to Household Food Security in the United States in 2015," Economic Research Service, USDA, September 2016, https://www.ers.usda.gov/publications/pub-details/?pubid=79430. Seniors are defined in this report as individuals aged 65 years and older.

8. National Foundation to End Senior Hunger (2014), "Spotlight on Senior Health: Adverse Health Outcomes of Food Insecure Older Americans," March 2014, http://www.nfesh.org/wp-content/uploads/2013/03/SeniorLiteratureReport-Final-Draft.pdf.

9. Census Bureau, 2008 and 2016 Current Population Survey's Annual Social and Economic Supplements.

10. Census Bureau, 2008 and 2016 Current Population Survey's Annual Social and Economic Supplements.

11. Census Bureau, 2014 National Population Projections.

12. Kelsey Farson Gray and Karen Cunnyngham, "Trends in Supplemental Nutrition Assistance Program Participation Rates: Fiscal Year 2010 to Fiscal Year 2014," Department of Agriculture, Office of Policy Support, June 2016, https://www.fns.usda.gov/snap/trends-supplemental-nutrition-assistance-program-participation-rates-fiscal-year-2010-fiscal-year.

13. James Ziliak and Craig Gundersen, "Food Insecurity Among Older Adults," AARP Foundation, August 2011, http://www.aarp.org/content/dam/aarp/aarp_foundation/pdf_2011/AARPFoundation_HungerReport_2011.pdf.

14. Census Bureau, 2011–2015 American Community Survey 5-Year Estimates.

15. Ibid.

EVALUATING THE AUTHOR'S ARGUMENTS:

The viewpoint author explores the rate of food insecurity among seniors in the US. Does it appear that enough is being done to help this population? Why might some seniors go without government help, according to the author? What could be done about this?

Viewpoint 5

Food Insecurity Is Linked to Major Chronic Diseases

"Not everyone has easy access to opportunities that can help them reduce their risk of disease."

Susan Perry

In the following viewpoint, Susan Perry looks more closely at some of the health problems that can result from food insecurity. One study reveals that food insecurity is closely linked to 10 common health problems. Other research has suggested that people living in poverty may need to choose between buying food and buying medicine. People in poverty are also less likely to have health insurance. Together these factors lead to a variety of health problems for people in poverty. Susan Perry writes about consumer health for *MinnPost*, an online publication for Minnesota.

AS YOU READ, CONSIDER THE FOLLOWING QUESTIONS:
1. How is food insecurity related to 10 common diseases?
2. How is income related to these diseases?
3. Why didn't people in the study buy enough fresh produce?

"Food Insecurity Linked to 10 Major Chronic Diseases," by Susan Perry, *MinnPost*, August 2, 2017. Reprinted by permission.

Some politicians, pundits—and, presumably, members of the public—like to blame sick people for their poor health.

As Rep. Mo Brooks, R-Alabama, famously—or infamously—stated while arguing for his party's failed replacement of the Affordable Care Act, "[Trumpcare] will allow insurance companies to require people who have higher health care costs to contribute more to the insurance pool that helps offset all these costs, thereby reducing the cost to those people who lead good lives; they're healthy, they've done the things to keep their bodies healthy."

I'm not sure what Brooks means by "doing things to keep their bodies healthy," but if he means they don't smoke, exercise regularly, eat plenty of fruits and veggies, and maintain a healthy weight (the four most basic tenets of preventive health), well, plenty of people who do all those things develop chronic and even life-threatening illnesses. Having healthy habits only reduces your risk of becoming seriously ill. It doesn't guarantee anything.

Brooks' statement also seems to presume that "keeping the body healthy" is an equally doable task for everyone. And that is simply not the case. Not everyone has easy access to opportunities that can help them reduce their risk of disease.

A Strong Predictor of Disease

That reality is underscored in a new study on food insecurity and health released this week by the US Department of Agriculture (USDA). It found that low food security—difficulty with consistently obtaining access to adequate amounts of healthy, affordable food—is associated among working-age adults with an increased risk of 10 of the most common, costly and preventable chronic conditions, including high blood pressure (hypertension), coronary heart disease (CHD), hepatitis, stroke, cancer, arthritis, chronic obstructive pulmonary disease (COPD) and kidney disease.

Poor nutrition is believed to play a direct role in many of those conditions.

In fact, the study found that, in some cases, the level of a person's food security was an even greater predictor of chronic illness than income. "Income is significantly associated with only 3 of the 10 chronic diseases—hepatitis, arthritis, and COPD—while

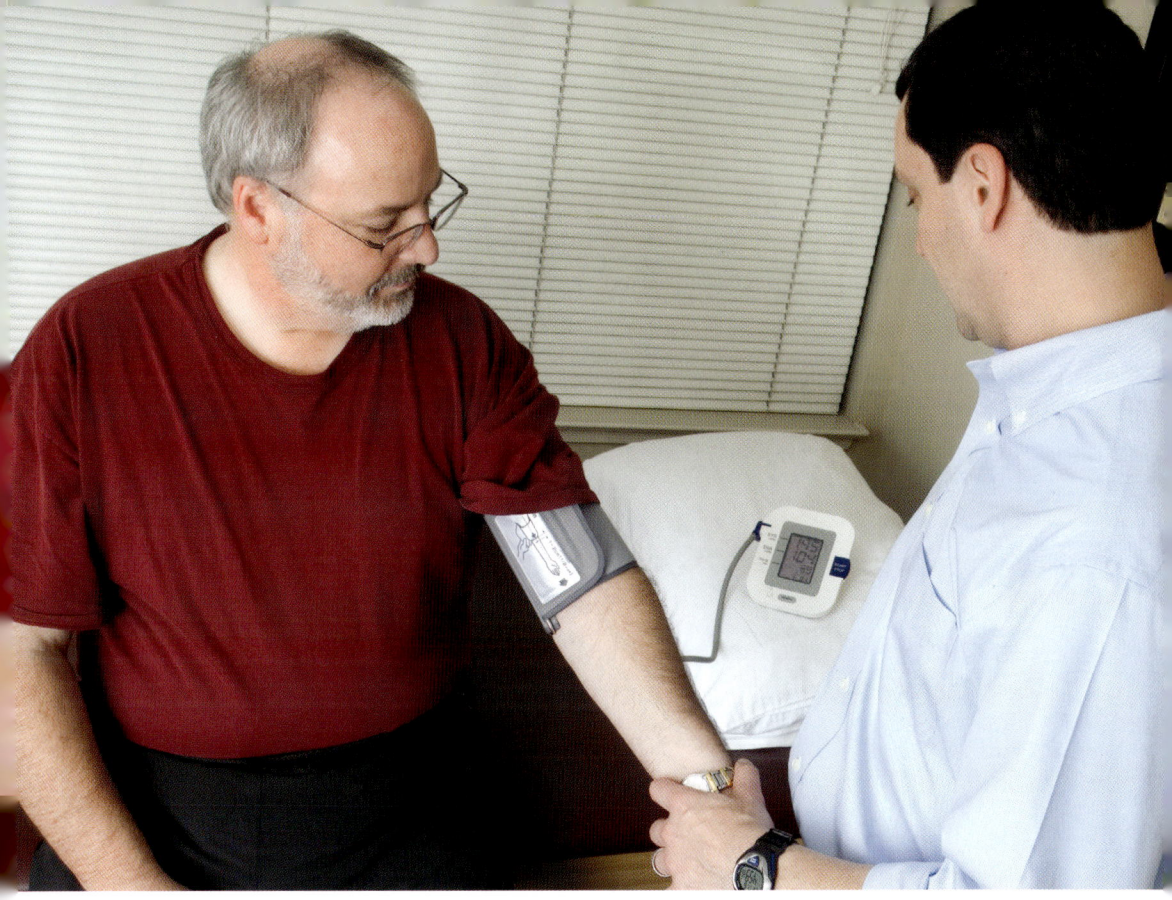

Food insecurity is directly tied to several serious chronic conditions that negatively affect health and well-being.

food insecurity is significantly associated with all 10," the study's authors write.

Furthermore, as food insecurity worsens, the likelihood of having each of these conditions increases.

Millions of Americans live in food-insecure households. The USDA estimates that 12.7 percent (15.8 million) of US households were food insecure—had difficulty getting enough healthy food to eat—at some point during 2015. At least 5.0 percent (6.3 million) of US households had very low food security that year.

Study Details

The USDA study used five years of data (2011-2015) from the National Health Interview Survey, which includes a demographically representative sample of about 40,000 US households. Based

> **FAST FACT**
> The USDA estimated that 12.7 percent (15.8 million) of US households were food insecure at some point during 2015. At least 5.0 percent (6.3 million) of US households had very low food security that year.

on answers to questions designed to assess food security, the USDA researchers were able to categorize each of the surveyed households as having either high, marginal, low or very low food security.

According to the data, people who live in households with low food security tend to be older, less educated and more likely to lack health insurance than those in households where food security is not an issue. The study also found that as food insecurity worsens, the heads of those households are more likely to be unemployed—and unmarried. Racial inequities are also part of the picture: Blacks and Hispanics are more likely than whites and Asian-Americans to live in households with low or very low food security.

Here are some other findings from the study:
- Adults in households with very low food security were 15 percentage points more likely to have a chronic illness than adults in households with high food security.
- The number of chronic conditions for adults in households with low food security was, on average, 18 percent higher than for those in high food-secure households.
- As food security worsened, the prevalence of chronic illness increased. For example, the prevalence of diagnosed high blood pressure was 19.7 percent among households with high food security, 23.6 percent among those with marginal food security, 28 percent among those with low food security and 36.1 percent among those with very low food security.
- Adults in households with marginal food security were 9 percentage points less likely to report excellent health, compared to those in households with high food security.

This particular study didn't examine why food insecurity is linked to poorer health outcomes, but previous research has found that low-income households often have to make trade-offs between food and other health-related necessities, such as buying medications.

Being able to easily access—and afford—healthy foods are also factors. As a 2012 study of food insecurity in the Twin Cities reported, food-insecure households are significantly more likely to serve processed and sugar-laden foods to their families and less likely to serve fresh fruits and vegetables.

The reason cited by study's participants: good-quality fresh produce was too expensive or too difficult to find in their neighborhood to purchase regularly.

Change Not Blame

The USDA study reports only a correlation between food insecurity and a greater risk of chronic disease. It doesn't prove there is a direct link between the two. Other factors are certainly also involved.

Still, it's clear from this and other research that we need to stop blaming people for being sick and start finding ways—on the societal, not just on the individual level—to help them be healthier.

EVALUATING THE AUTHOR'S ARGUMENTS:

Viewpoint author Susan Perry argues that food security is closely tied to health. What factors appear to lead to health problems for people in poverty? How could they be addressed? Is this an individual problem, a community problem, or a government problem?

Chapter 2

What Causes Food Insecurity?

There are several reasons behind a lack of food security around the world.

Viewpoint 1

We Must Curb Population Growth

Population Connection

"The burden of high food prices falls disproportionately on the poor, who spend 60–80 percent of their incomes on food."

In the following viewpoint, Population Connection explores how high population growth affects food security. The author argues that, while several factors threaten global food security, population growth is the most significant factor. As the global population grows, the demand for more food means more land and water must be devoted to food production. However, farming may not be able to keep up. This could lead to growing hunger and more children suffering from malnutrition. Population Connection is a nonprofit organization that raises awareness of population challenges.

AS YOU READ, CONSIDER THE FOLLOWING QUESTIONS:
1. What does stunted growth in children mean?
2. What factors contribute to global food security?
3. Why is it hard for food production to keep up with population growth?

"Population Growth and Food Insecurity," Population Connection, January 28, 2015. Reprinted by permission.

In 2011, drought struck the Horn of Africa, sparking widespread food shortages. An estimated 13 million people in Somalia, Ethiopia, and Kenya faced persistent hunger, which killed between 50,000 and 100,000 people—half of whom were children under five.

According to UN Emergency Relief Coordinator, Valerie Amos, it was East Africa's "driest period in 60 years," and it left people "increasingly unable to cope." Amos states that pre-existing problems in the region, including "insecurity and conflict, population growth, poverty, and over-utilization of land" only compounded the effects of the drought.

The situation was especially dire in Somalia, where the UN declared famine. (The UN defines famine as malnutrition rates above 30 percent; at least 20 percent of households facing extreme food shortages; and a mortality rate over 2 people per 10,000 per day.) Nearly 10 million people in the Horn of Africa are still food insecure, following the drought.

Somali women have an average of 6.61 births over the course of their reproductive lives. One in 11 infants dies before his or her first birthday. One in seven dies before turning five. Despite high rates of infant and child mortality, Somalia has a population growth rate of 2.87 percent; at that rate its population will double every 24 years, making food security that much farther out of reach.

Undernutrition has led to the stunted growth of 165 million children worldwide, and is responsible for 45 percent of child deaths in low- and middle-income countries (LMICs). In LMICs, 27 percent of all babies are born small for their gestational age, which contributes to a quarter of newborn deaths. "Stunted doesn't mean simply short," says Anthony Lake, executive director of UNICEF. "The child's brain never properly develops. Irrevocably. That's it. You can't fix it later. You can fix being underweight. You can't fix being stunted after age 2. What this means is, for the remainder of that child's life, irrevocably the child will learn less in school, will earn less later, is more vulnerable to disease. This is a tragic violation of that child's life, but it's also a tremendous strain on that society."

In some parts of the world, including some regions of Africa, famine is brought on by climate and land factors, government conflicts, and overpopulation.

Where Hunger Strikes

Hunger kills more people than AIDS, malaria, and tuberculosis combined. According to Hilary Benn, UK Secretary of State for Environment, Food and Rural Affairs, in less arable or poorly-governed parts of the world, "a perfect storm" of factors threaten global food security: rising prices, drought and other climate disasters, arable land shortages, and increasing demand. The most significant contributor to increasing demand is a population that's climbing toward 9.6 billion in 2050.

FAO estimates that there are 868 million undernourished people, 98 percent of whom live in the developing world. The good news is that the number decreased from 1.23 billion in 2009, when food prices spiked. The bad news is that one in eight people still go to bed hungry each night. Experts say it is possible to meet the Millennium

Development Goal of halving the proportion of people who suffer from hunger by 2015; however, it will take extensive effort in order to get there. While some countries have made significant progress, 15 percent of people in the developing world remain undernourished.

Sub-Saharan Africa has the highest proportion of undernourished people in any region; there, one in four are chronically hungry. Reflecting population growth and rising food insecurity, the number of hungry people on the African continent rose by 20 million from 2007 to 2010-2012.

According to WFP, the levels of food insecurity in Egypt have risen significantly over the past three years, as Egypt faces its worst economic crisis since the 1930s. In 2011, 13.7 million Egyptians—17 percent of the population—experienced food insecurity, and 31 percent of children under five experienced stunted growth. Experts claim statistics have only gotten worse since data was last collected. "As the economic situation grows gloomier and more people have been forced into poverty, we can only imagine that this number has grown," says Abeer Etefa, of the WFP's Middle East and North Africa office.

Rising Food Prices, Failing Harvests

Over the last decade, food prices worldwide have risen twice as fast as inflation. Political instability can incite full-blown food crises in food-insecure regions. In DRC, ongoing conflicts have caused the undernourished population to jump from 26 percent in 1990–1992 to 70 percent in 2011. One in four children there are malnourished.

The burden of high food prices falls disproportionately on the poor, who spend 60–80 percent of their incomes on food. Women, children, and the elderly fare the worst when food is scarce. According to Biraj Patnaik, food advisor to the Indian government, "Women often, given the gender inequity in our society, ration their own food so they can feed the children and feed parents." This is a pattern that plays out across the developing world.

In industrialized countries, farmers have been able to increase crop production when necessary; for example, they raised cereal outputs by 10 percent in 2009 during the global food crisis. But a recent report by the OECD and FAO estimates that growth in agricultural productivity will slow to just 1.7 percent annually over the next decade.

Failing harvests in the US, Ukraine, and other countries have eroded reserves to their lowest level since 1974. "We've not been producing as much as we are consuming. Supplies are now very tight across the world and reserves are at a very low level, leaving no room for unexpected events next year," says Abdolreza Abbassian, a senior economist at FAO.

> **FAST FACT**
> Poor nutrition has led to the stunted growth of 165 million children worldwide. It is responsible for 45 percent of child deaths in low- and middle-income countries.

A number of strategies have successfully raised food production in the developing world as well, most notably the Green Revolution in India, Mexico, and to some extent, the Philippines. But in 2008, a World Bank and FAO study found that large production increases made possible through science and technology during the last 30 years have actually not improved food security for the poorest people. The study spanned six years and included the testimonies of about 400 international agricultural experts.

Rising Demand

The African population is projected to more than double by the middle of this century, adding 1.3 billion people despite the ravages of hunger, disease, and civil conflict.

FAO economist Kostas Stamoulis says that "cereal yields in developing countries will need to increase by 40 percent, irrigation water requirements will rise by up to 50 percent, and some 100–200 million hectares of additional land may be needed" in order to meet rising demand.

Just to keep up with rising demand (not to improve the current situation), FAO estimates that overall food production must increase by 70 percent by 2050. "We're going to have to produce more food in the next 40 years than we have in the last 10,000," says William G. Lesher, former chief economist for the USDA. "Some people say we'll just add more land or more water. But we're not going to do much of either." That's because the low-hanging fruit has already been picked, so to speak. "The easy things have been done," says Nina V. Fedoroff, a biotechnology expert at Pennsylvania State University. "The problems that are left are hard." Researchers estimate that it would take five times the earth's current resources to meet the needs of a global population consuming at a rate equivalent to that of the United States today.

Long-Term Solution

Agricultural innovation and more equitable food distribution would reduce rates of undernourishment on our overworked planet. But a crucial part of ending the "perfect storm" is population stabilization. Tim Dyson, agriculture expert at the London School of Economics, says, "We tend to deal with what is happening now, today, tomorrow or next week. Insufficient attention is given to more fundamental processes such as population growth, or the need to invest in agriculture research for people living in difficult environments."

EVALUATING THE AUTHOR'S ARGUMENTS:

In this viewpoint, the Population Connection argues that we need to put a halt to population growth in order to keep up with food demands. Do you think that is possible? Why or why not? How might we go about it? Are there other answers?

Viewpoint 2

Don't Blame Population Growth

Joe Hasell

"The number of people dying due to famine in recent decades is only a tiny fraction of that in previous eras."

In the following viewpoint, Joe Hasell challenges the view that population growth is to blame for food insecurity. The author notes that as population has grown, the number of people dying from famine has shrunk. Even when looking at individual countries, this generally holds true. Other factors contributing to hunger include violence, poor access to markets, and inequality. Joe Hasell leads research projects on topics such as famine and war for Our World in Data, which uses data to understand the world's problems.

AS YOU READ, CONSIDER THE FOLLOWING QUESTIONS:
1. What factors prevent food from getting to people in need, according to the viewpoint?
2. How does a famine differ from normal circumstances that include hunger and malnutrition?
3. Do countries with high population growth typically also have a high number of people who don't get enough food?

"Does Population Growth Lead to Hunger and Famine?" by Joe Hasell, Our World in Data, April 3, 2018. https://ourworldindata.org/population-growth-and-famines. Licensed under CC BY 4.0 International.

It's no good blaming climate change or food shortages or political corruption. Sorry to be neo-Malthusian about it, but continuing population growth in this region makes periodic famine unavoidable... Many of the children saved by the money raised over the next few weeks will inevitably be back again in similar feeding centres with their own children in a few years time.
—Blog entry from British environmentalist Sir Jonathan Porritt, 11/07/2011[1]

It is not uncommon to see arguments along the lines of this quote from Sir Jonathan Porritt, claiming that famines are ultimately caused by overpopulation. Porritt—former director of "Friends of the Earth" and also former chairman of the UK Government's Sustainable Development Commission—was talking about the 2011 famine in Somalia that went on to kill roughly 250,000 people.[2] He seems certain that the rapid population growth witnessed in East Africa had made famine there "unavoidable."

There is something compelling about this logic: a finite land area, with a limited "carrying capacity," cannot continue to feed a growing population indefinitely. From such a perspective, the provision of humanitarian aid to famine-afflicted countries, however well intended, represents only a temporary fix. In this view it fails to address the fundamental issue: there simply being too many mouths to feed.

As mentioned in the quote, this suggestion is commonly associated with the name of Thomas Robert Malthus, the English political economist writing at the turn of the nineteenth century. Malthus is famous for the assertion that in the absence of "preventative checks" to reduce birth rates, the natural tendency for populations to increase—being "so superior to the power of the earth to produce subsistence for man"—ultimately results in "positive checks" that increase the death rate. If all else fails to curb population, "gigantic inevitable famine stalks in the rear, and with one mighty blow levels the population with the food of the world."[3]

But does the evidence support this idea? Here we look into the relationship between population growth and famine, as well as that between population growth and hunger more generally.

Famine Victims Worldwide

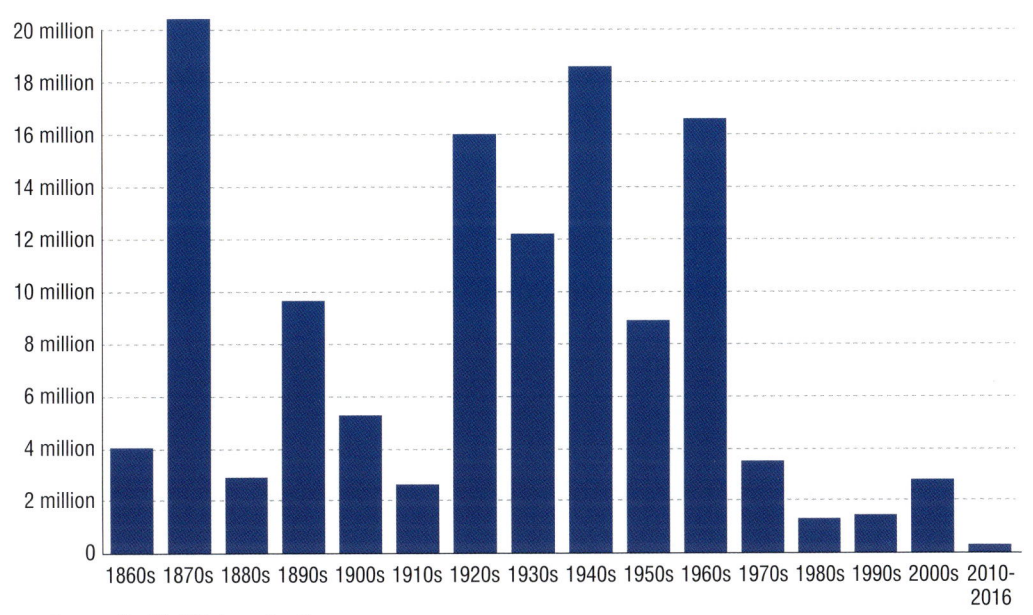

[Bar chart showing famine victims by decade from 1860s to 2010-2016. Approximate values: 1860s ~4 million; 1870s ~20+ million; 1880s ~3 million; 1890s ~9.5 million; 1900s ~5 million; 1910s ~2.5 million; 1920s ~16 million; 1930s ~12 million; 1940s ~18.5 million; 1950s ~9 million; 1960s ~16.5 million; 1970s ~3.5 million; 1980s ~1.2 million; 1990s ~1.3 million; 2000s ~3 million; 2010-2016 ~0.3 million.]

Source: OurWorldData.org/familes

Does Population Growth Cause Famine?

This chart compares the number of famine deaths per decade—based on our famine dataset—with the world population over the same period.

Looking at the world as whole, it is very difficult to square Malthus' hypothesis with the simple but stark fact that, despite the world's population increasing from less than one billion in 1800 to more than seven billion today, the number of people dying due to famine in recent decades is only a tiny fraction of that in previous eras.

We might naturally think that the explanation for this trend lies in increasing agricultural production. Indeed, food supply per person has consistently increased in recent decades. The large increase in global population being met with an even greater increase in food supply (largely due to increases in yields per hectare).

However, looking at the issue in this way is too simple. As we discuss in our entry on Famines, insufficient aggregate food supply per person is just one factor that can bring about famine mortality. Contemporary famine scholarship tends to suggest that insufficient aggregate food supply is less important than one might think, and

What Causes Food Insecurity?

instead emphasises the role of public policy and violence: in most famines of the 20th and 21st centuries, conflict, political oppression, corruption, or gross economic mismanagement on the part of dictatorships or colonial regimes played a key role.[4]

The same also applies for the most acutely food-insecure countries today.[5]

It is also true of the 2011 famine in Somalia referred to above, in which food aid was greatly restricted, and in some cases diverted, by militant Islamist group al Shabaab and other armed opposition groups in the country.[6]

Famine scholar Stephen Devereux of the Institute of Development Studies, University of Sussex, summarizes the trajectory of famines over the 20th century as follows: "The achievement of a global capacity to guarantee food security was accompanied by a simultaneous expansion of the capacity of governments to inflict lethal policies, including genocidal policies often involving the extraction of food from the poor and denial of food to the starving."[7]

Thus, all in all, the recent history of famine mortality does not fit the Malthusian narrative particularly well. Firstly, contrary to what Malthus predicted for rapidly increasing populations, food supply per person has—in all regions—increased as populations have grown. Secondly, famines have not become more, but less frequent. Thirdly, in the modern era the occurrence of major famine mortality, and its prevention, is something for which politics and policy seem the more salient triggers.

Does Population Growth Increase Hunger?

Famines tend to be thought of as acute periods of crisis, and are in that sense to be distinguished from more chronic manifestations of hunger that may in some places represent "normal" circumstances, despite being responsible for large numbers of deaths.[8]

Given the typically political nature of outbreaks of such famine crises, it may make more sense to look for an effect of population growth on the longer-term trends of hunger and malnutrition.

But again, at the global level, we know that population growth has been accompanied by a downward trend in hunger. As we discuss in our entry on Hunger and Undernourishment, in recent decades the

The relationship between population and hunger is complicated. High population growth doesn't always lead to higher levels of hunger.

proportion of undernourished people in the world has fallen, and, although more muted, this fall is also seen in the absolute number. The number of people dying globally due to insufficient calorie or protein intake has also fallen, from almost half a million in the 1990s to roughly 300,000 in the most recent data.

Within Countries

We can also look at the experiences of individual countries, rather than just at the global level. Do those countries with particularly high population growth rates find it harder to adequately feed its population?

In order to get some idea about this, we can compare countries' Global Hunger Index (GHI) score with their population growth rates. GHI is a composite measure, out of 100, that combines four indicators: undernourishment, child wasting, child stunting, and child mortality.[9]

The first scoring was conducted in 1992, and was then repeated every eight years with the most recent being in carried out in 2017. The score is based on data collected in the years leading up to the scoring year, and as such reflect the hunger levels in this period rather than solely capturing conditions in the year itself. All the countries for which there was GHI data available between 1992 and 2017 [were included].[10] Crucially, this excludes a number of very food-insecure countries including the Democratic Republic of Congo, South Sudan and Somalia, which have also seen high levels of population growth.[11] This should be borne in mind when interpreting the following results.

Of the countries for which we do have GHI data, it is clear that those with higher levels of hunger have also tended to have had higher population growth over the last 25 years.[12]

It is important to see though that among the countries for which we have GHI scores in both 1992 and 2017, the level of hunger went down in all but one—Iraq. Over the same period population went up in almost every case. Moreover, those countries that experienced higher levels of population growth in fact saw a bigger drop in their GHI score over this period.[13]

The countries that saw high population growth over this period started with higher levels of hunger in 1992. So what we are seeing here is that countries are converging towards lower levels of hunger: it fell quickest in countries with the highest levels of hunger.

So whilst countries that experience hunger do tend to have high levels of population growth, the idea that population growth necessarily leads to increased hunger is clearly mistaken: many countries with high population growth have recently managed to decrease levels of hunger substantially.

Population Growth Does Not Make Famine Inevitable

Environmental degradation, including climate change, does pose a threat to food security, and the growth of human populations has undoubtedly exacerbated many environmental pressures. However,

FAST FACT
Global Hunger Index (GHI) is a measure that combines four indicators: undernourishment, child wasting, child stunting, and child mortality. GHI has been falling in most countries, even those with high population growth.

this represents only one aspect of the complex explanation of why so many people suffer and die from undernourishment today, despite their being adequate food available for consumption globally.[14]

"Malthusian" explanations of famine and hunger thus fall short for the following reasons, the evidence for which we reviewed above:

- Per capita food supply has increased as populations have grown, largely due to increasing yields.
- Famine deaths have decreased, not increased, with population growth.
- Food scarcity has played a smaller role in famines than suggested by the Malthusian narrative. It ignores other factors like conflict, poverty, access to markets, healthcare systems, and political institutions.
- Population growth is high where hunger is high, but that does not mean that population growth makes hunger inevitable. On the contrary, we see that hunger has fallen fastest in countries with high population growth.

If we want to put an end to hunger, we need to understand the diverse causes that bring it about. Oversimplifications that mistakenly see hunger and famine as an inevitable consequence of population growth do not contribute to this end.

References

1. Who would have thought it? Population growth and famine would appear to be linked! Blog entry from www.jonathanporritt.com, dated 11/07/2011. Accessed 19 Jan 2018. Emphasis added.

2. The excess mortality estimate is taken from the World Peace Foundation list of famines.

3. Malthus T.R. 1798. *An Essay on the Principle of Population*. Chapter VII, p 44.

4. See, for instance, de Waal, A. The end of famine? Prospects for the elimination of mass starvation by political action, *Political Geography*, 62:2008.

5. The threat of famine in Yemen, South Sudan and Nigeria are all the direct consequence of conflict, and the drought in Somalia arrives after decades of conflict and political instability. See FEWS.net for more details.

6. Seal, A., & Bailey, R. (2013). The 2011 Famine in Somalia: lessons learnt from a failed response? *Conflict and Health*, 7, 22. http://doi.org/10.1186/1752-1505-7-22. As the authors note, this was in part due to concern on the part of humanitarian organisations that they would be contravening US government sanctions. Furthermore, both the US and the EU had significantly reduced humanitarian spending in the country in the run up to the famine.

7. Devereux, S. *Famine in the Twentieth Century.* IDS working paper 105, 2000.

8. de Waal, 2018 defines famine as "a crisis of mass hunger that causes elevated mortality over a specific period of time." Note that the official IPC classification system used by the UN for famine declarations just looks at total (undernourishment-related) death rates in absolute terms, rather than relative to any non-crisis reference level. This contrasts somewhat to the typical ex-ante famine assessment in which excess mortality is estimated by factoring out the counterfactual death rate—however high.

9. More information on these individual indicators, including their definitions, can be found on our entry on Hunger and Undernourishment.

10. Population data was taken from the World Bank for 1992 to 2016. Note that GHI is typically not collected for wealthy countries. Below a score of 5, GHI gets bottom coded as "<5." Of the 95 countries for which we have data in both years, none of them began bottom coded but five moved into this range by 2017. In the analysis that follows we replaced these bottom-coded observations with a GHI of 2.5. However the key results are robust to omitting these countries altogether. As a robustness check, we also conducted the analysis on the prevalence of undernourishment separately (one of the four components of GHI). The key results remained unchanged.

11. These three countries would be situated in the top quarter of our sample in terms of population growth, with DRC and South Sudan roughly in the top decile.

12. Statistically significant at the 1% level, even when controlling for GDP per capita in 2016 (using World Bank PPP data).

13. This relationship is significant at the 1% level. The relationship is stronger (both in magnitude and significance) controlling for GDP per capita (using World Bank PPP data).

14. World food supply per person is higher than the Average Dietary Energy Requirements of all countries. See our entry on Food per Person for more details.

EVALUATING THE AUTHOR'S ARGUMENTS:

Viewpoint author Joe Hasell contends that population growth is not the only or primary reason for hunger. How does his argument compare to the previous viewpoint? Which factors seem most important to you now? Can we forget about trying to control population growth? Why or why not?

Viewpoint 3

Tackle Climate Change to Improve Food Security

"Climate change affects food production and availability, access, quality, utilization, and stability of food systems."

Concern Worldwide US

In the following viewpoint, authors from Concern Worldwide US explore how climate change threatens food security. Concern Worldwide US, a global humanitarian organization, notes that while the percentage of people going hungry has shrunk, the total number of people has grown as the population grows. Countries with high levels of hunger are often also the most vulnerable to climate change. Concern Worldwide is a humanitarian agency that engages in long-term development work to help the world's poorest people.

AS YOU READ, CONSIDER THE FOLLOWING QUESTIONS:
1. Who is hurt most when climate change disasters interfere with food production and distribution?
2. In what various ways does climate change affect the availability of food?
3. How does climate change affect the nutrition of foods?

"How Climate Change Threatens Food Security—and Why We're All at Risk," Concern Worldwide US, Inc, October 23, 2019. Reprinted by permission.

For hungry and undernourished people, climate change is a threat multiplier. Since the early 1990s, the number of extreme weather-related disasters has doubled. This has reduced the yields of major crops and contributed to an increase in food prices and a decrease in income.

These disasters have also disproportionately harmed low-income people and their access to food, which is why we have chosen to focus on the connection between climate change and food security in the 2019 Global Hunger Index (GHI), prepared by Concern Worldwide and Welthungerhilfe. Sadly, this is not a trend that appears to be going away any time soon. Looking ahead, climate models predict higher average temperatures in most land and ocean regions, hotter extremes in many inhabited regions, and both heavy precipitation and an increasing probability of drought in some areas. These are all additional challenges for reducing hunger.

While the world has made gradual progress in reducing hunger on a global scale since 2000, this progress has been uneven. We've reduced global hunger, but in absolute terms, the number of people going to bed hungry is on the rise. The GHI takes into account the rates of undernourishment, child stunting, child wasting, and child mortality to highlight where action is most needed to fight hunger. With 2019's data now available (along with an updated ranking of the world's hungriest countries), let's take a look at some of the ways climate change threatens food security—and how that may impact all of us.

Climate Change and Food Security: Fast Facts

- Climate change is a threat multiplier for hungry and under-nourished people.
- Countries with high levels of hunger are often also highly vulnerable to climate change, and have a low capacity to adapt.
- Climate change affects food production and availability, access, quality, utilization, and stability of food systems. In short, it impacts all aspects of the food system.
- Extreme weather-related disasters are increasing and reduce the yields of major crops.

Climate change and extreme weather conditions, such as the drought that decimated this corn crop, can contribute to food insecurity.

- Higher levels of CO2 reduce the nutritional value of crops.
- The global food system contributes about one-third of greenhouse gas emissions. About ⅔ of food are lost and wasted from farm to table. These losses therefore exacerbate climate change without improving food security or nutrition.
- Climate change and conflict combined destroy livelihoods, drive displacement, widen inequalities, and undermine sustainable development.
- Ending hunger and undernutrition in a changing climate demands large-scale action.

Climate Change Threatens Agriculture and Food Production

Higher temperatures, water scarcity, extreme events like droughts and floods, and greater CO2 concentrations in the atmosphere have already begun to impact staple crops around the world. Maize and wheat production has declined in recent years due to extreme weather events, plant diseases, and an overall increase in water scarcity.

According to the Food and Agriculture Organization of the United Nations, the unpredictable yield for cereal crops in semi-arid

> **FAST FACT**
> Roughly one-third of the food produced by farmers in low- and middle-income countries is lost between the field and the market. In high-income countries, a similar amount is wasted between the market and the table.

regions of the world (like the Sahel region of Africa) is at least 80% the result of climate variability.

In other areas like Bangladesh and Vietnam, rising sea levels pose a different threat to food security. As the saltwater is more likely to flood coastal farmlands, it is also more likely to kill off rice crops. Half of Vietnam's national rice production is centered on the Mekong Delta region, which means that a flood in this region (roughly the size of Maryland) could impact both the country's food security and economy.

While the causes of these issues are fairly consistent (and often not the doing of the people living in these regions), the solutions are not. This means that, with the effects of climate change already apparent in areas like the Horn of Africa and Southeast Asia, we need to find unique methods to mitigate disasters when they strike, and develop bespoke ways to reduce the impacts of hazards on the lives and livelihoods of these areas in the future.

Climate Change Limits Food Access

If climate change affects food production, it stands to reason that it also affects food access. This simple supply-and-demand has big impacts: Climate change and weather disasters (such as floods or drought) can lead to inflated prices for the food that is available. These price spikes leave the poorest households (urban poor and rural food-buyers) most vulnerable, with the urban poor spending up to 75% of their total budget on food alone.

Because our food systems are increasingly dependent on one another, this means that more frequent and more extreme events in one region could disrupt clusters of food systems—even the global food system as a whole. The areas least likely to adjust to a sudden event or shock, however, continue to be the ones disproportionately affected.

Climate Change Decreases Nutrition and Nutritional Value

In many food-insecure areas, the next concern becomes nutrition. In low-income and agrarian communities, the patterns of food consumption are seasonal. A pre-harvest "lean season" will leave families reducing their food consumption (often skipping one or more meals each day) until the next harvest. With climate change reducing harvests, this means that the lean period may be extended if there are fewer supplies, or if it takes longer to get an adequate harvest.

Alternatively, climate change can adversely affect the nutritional value of food that is grown. Studies show that higher carbon dioxide concentrations reduce the protein, zinc, and iron content of crops. By 2050, an estimated additional 175 million people could have zinc deficiencies (which can, among other things, make them more susceptible to illnesses) and an additional 122 million people could be protein deficient. Communities relying largely on plant harvests for their nutrition will, again, feel this most acutely.

Beyond plant-based nutrition, this also has a ripple effect on livestock, who rely on the same resources as humans to eat, grow, and produce meat and/or milk. Livestock are also severely threatened by drought, accounting for 36% of drought-related losses (crops account for 49%). Climate extremes also threaten fish populations, especially in areas like Southeast Asia.

Climate Change Increases Food Waste

Rain doesn't guarantee healthy crops, either. Higher rainfalls or flooding can produce toxic mold on crops. Crops grown in high-drought areas that are then moved into humid storage facilities are vulnerable to fungal infections or pests. The more climate changes and the more that extreme climate events become commonplace, the more food we lose on an annual basis.

According to the UN's Food and Agriculture Organization, roughly one-third of the food produced by farmers is lost between the field and the market in low- and middle-income countries. In high-income countries, a similar amount is wasted between the market and the table. Currently, the food system contributes 21–37%

of greenhouse gases, meaning that these food losses add to the climate crisis but do nothing for food security or malnutrition levels.

Conclusion

Climate change affects the global food system in such a way that those who already suffer from hunger and undernutrition are those most vulnerable to these added threats. In order to end hunger—as is one of our top Sustainable Development Goals for the year 2030—we therefore need to also tackle the current climate crisis, particularly the topic of climate justice and the inequities that are raised by climate change.

As we can see with the increasingly global nature of our food system, however, this cannot happen in isolation. We must foster global solidarity with the most climate-vulnerable communities and countries, with high-income countries (especially those with the highest greenhouse emissions) taking responsibility for both mitigating the causes of climate change and supporting low- and middle-income countries in adapting to the effects of these changes. All of this is a tall order, but it's an order that will affect all of our futures, regardless of where we live.

EVALUATING THE AUTHOR'S ARGUMENTS:

Climate change is having the worst effects on low-income countries. Viewpoint author Concern Worldwide argues that high-income countries should take the lead in slowing climate change. What reasoning does the author give? Do you agree? Why or why not?

Viewpoint 4

College Students Need More Help

Emily Moon

"Colleges of all kinds have stigmatized or overlooked the needs of low-income students, who make up a fast-growing portion of the nation's student body."

In the following viewpoint, Emily Moon examines the problem of college students who suffer from food insecurity. The author argues that college food pantries may not be easily accessible, and even when they are, some students are too embarrassed to use them. In any case, food pantries alone are not enough to supply the need. Some government aid is available, but students don't always know when they are eligible. Others aren't eligible because they can't get work-study jobs or don't have the time to work 20 hours a week, as the program requires. Emily Moon is a staff writer at Pacific Standard.

"Half of College Students Are Food Insecure. Are Universities Doing Enough to Help Them?" by Emily Moon, The Social Justice Foundation, June 17, 2019. Reprinted by permission.

AS YOU READ, CONSIDER THE FOLLOWING QUESTIONS:
1. How do tuition and housing prices contribute to food insecurity?
2. How are college students rallying to demand more support?
3. Why do work requirements for college students make it hard for many to use the SNAP program?

Nearly half of America's college students can't afford their next meal. On many campuses, these students—who are getting by on donated meal swipes and sometimes living out of their cars—also face another barrier to food security: The people in power don't believe them.

"So many folks want to deny that this is a problem," says Ruben Canedo, who heads the food insecurity efforts at the University of California–Berkeley. "They don't consider the college population a population that is struggling with their food and housing."

Despite its prevalence, food insecurity on college campuses has largely been a hidden problem; colleges of all kinds have stigmatized or overlooked the needs of low-income students, who make up a fast-growing portion of the nation's student body. One Oregon State University student says she was getting all her groceries from the Dollar Tree this week. Another asked a case manager at the University of California–Davis for help during finals, saying she'd be living in her car this summer.

While hundreds of universities have opened food pantries since 2009, food insecurity made it into the national conversation much more recently. A reckoning that began with student activism has now led to policy changes, due in part to national attention from lawmakers—and an increasing demand for programs that go beyond establishing food pantries for hungry students.

In December of 2018, the United States Government Accountability Office called on Congress to make changes that would help more college students get benefits from the Supplemental Nutrition Assistance Program. Then just this month, a groundbreaking study from the non-profit research organization the Hope Center for College, Community, and Justice confirmed what many

Many college campuses offer food pantries in an effort to address food insecurity among their student populations.

universities had found from their own surveys: Forty-five percent of college students say they have experienced food insecurity in the last month, meaning they often skipped meals or couldn't afford to buy food when their groceries ran out.

Although many colleges already have food banks or basic needs centers, campus food insecurity is getting worse. "It's escalating as we start seeing higher prices for tuition, higher prices for housing, and changing demographics," says Leslie Kemp, director of Aggie Compass, the basic needs center at UC–Davis.

"We have right now the lowest purchasing power of financial aid for students, while having some of the highest costs of living across the country," Canedo says. "The financial equation is broken."

Since the GAO report came out, many leaders of programs addressing food insecurity say they have noticed renewed action on the issue. "This attention is very, very helpful," Kemp says. "It's

> **FAST FACT**
> A 2018 study found that 45 percent of college students said they had experienced food insecurity in the prior month.

bringing credibility to a problem that we've always had. It's getting around the myth that all college students eat ramen and all college students are broke."

The University of California–Irvine's student government declared a campus emergency over food security this month, setting aside $400,000 in one-time funds that will go toward hiring a case manager devoted to helping students with food or housing emergencies, the *Los Angeles Times* reports. At the University of Kentucky, a student group led a hunger strike in March to demand better resources for food insecurity. And in an email to the entire campus community last month, Oregon State University President Edward Ray wrote, "The crisis of food deprivation at Oregon State must end."

Program directors fighting food insecurity across the country applaud these gestures—and point to examples of real change that resulted from them. For example, Oregon State's faculty senate passed a resolution this year to include a section on every class syllabus that encourages students to reach out and get help from essential resources and that links to the Human Services Resource Center, according to Nicole Hindes, the center's assistant director. "We know this is a national problem, but there are so many [administrators] across the country that think their campus is somehow special," she says. "When administrators aren't listening, I think student activism is absolutely the place where that has to happen. It's important for us to listen to our students and believe them."

At UC schools, administrators have opened and coordinated basic needs centers on all nine campuses, according to Canedo. These centers help students apply to CalFresh (California's version of SNAP), negotiate their financial aid, and connect with case managers who can find them food and housing; some also offer free groceries. In 2018, 47 percent of respondents in the statewide undergraduate survey said they had "low" or "very low" food security.

In addition to more colleges opening needs centers, another solution to the problem could be informing students about SNAP, a federal program that gives low-income Americans money for groceries every month. Despite high demand, the program is underused on college campuses: Of the 3.3 million students who were eligible for the program in 2016, less than half said they participated, according to the 2018 GAO report.

Many of the basic needs directors would also like to see SNAP expanded. Most undocumented students can't get SNAP; others may not quite meet the income threshold. On top of that, the eligibility rules are "archaic," Hindes says. Generally, college students only qualify if they have a work-study job—but work-study funding hasn't kept up with need at the federal level. At OSU, Hindes says, more than half the students are eligible for work-study, but there's only enough funding for about 500. That makes it much harder for them to get SNAP. The alternative is working at least 20 hours a week, which research has shown can harm a student's focus and academic performance.

This is why UC–Davis now employs a county CalFresh representative to help students with their applications and conduct in-person interviews, which improve an applicant's chance at being approved. At other schools in the state, representatives make one visit per quarter.

But on many campuses, students default to the food pantry—often the most visible and most used food insecurity program. Even so, research shows many people avoid food pantries because of a persistent stigma. "It takes a great amount of courage to walk in the door," says Andrea Gutierrez, who oversees UC–Irvine's FRESH Basic Needs Hub.

Often, food pantries are inaccessible even when there's interest in using them. At the University of Missouri, students sometimes have trouble walking or biking to the food pantry, according to Tiger Pantry's director, Mathew Swan. When they do make it through the door, they have to fill out an order and wait for volunteers to hand them their groceries. "One of the biggest challenges is accessibility," he says.

Gutierrez and her staff have worked to make their food pantry feel accessible and open. The walls are a vibrant orange, the staff plays music so waiting in line isn't awkward, and there's a community kitchen where students can warm up their food. Most importantly, the center doesn't require students to prove need. "Many people call us a mini grocery store, and that was very intentional for us," she says. "We wanted to make sure that the shopping experience in a pantry would be similar to the shopping experience in a grocery store, to give dignity to our students who are showing up and asking for help."

Even the best campus food pantry is still an emergency response—most rely on donations or one-time student government funding—so many campuses are trying to fill the gaps with other solutions. UC–Davis opened its basic needs center last year, which combines all its services at one home base. Students can also download a new app that notifies them when leftover food from official catered events is available, a service that's been rolled out at several campuses across the country.

Overall, Canedo says, awareness of the issue is growing: When Berkeley's food pantry opened in 2014, it served 500 students a year. Now, it serves 5,000. Instead of one building and many disparate services, the campus now has a center where students can connect with a case manager for help on food and housing.

And yet, Canedo says, he still encounters critics who think he's prioritizing college students' hunger over others. They often ask, why are college students so important? "We're not doing this to establish a hierarchy of human value," he says. "College students are not more worthy or important than any other person. What we're saying is the better we support our college students, the better we're going to have professionals out in the community, taking care of the community."

EVALUATING THE AUTHOR'S ARGUMENTS:

This viewpoint author notes that some people question whether college students are a priority when it comes to hunger. Are there any factors that should be considered when dividing up limited resources? Why or why not? If so, what are the factors?

Viewpoint 5

Food Deserts Are Connected to Poor Health and Food Insecurity

"Studies have found that wealthy districts have three times as many supermarkets as poor ones do."

Food Empowerment Project

In the following viewpoint, Food Empowerment Project explains the concept of a food desert. Poor rural and urban communities may not have access to nearby grocery stores. People living in these communities get most of their food from convenience stores or fast-food restaurants. The selections there are often unhealthy and may be more expensive. These unhealthy diets contribute to several diseases and can lead to earlier death. Cities and activists are fighting to bring better options to food deserts. Food Empowerment Project is a nonprofit organization that seeks to create a more just and sustainable world by recognizing the power of one's food choices.

"Food Deserts," Food Empowerment Project. Reprinted by permission.

AS YOU READ, CONSIDER THE FOLLOWING QUESTIONS:
1. Why might people in urban areas struggle to buy food?
2. How are food deserts connected to race?
3. Which is typically more expensive, healthy food or unhealthy food?

Food deserts can be described as geographic areas where residents' access to affordable, healthy food options (especially fresh fruits and vegetables) is restricted or nonexistent due to the absence of grocery stores within convenient travelling distance. For instance, according to a report prepared for Congress by the Economic Research Service of the US Department of Agriculture, about 2.3 million people (or 2.2 percent of all US households) live more than one mile away from a supermarket and do not own a car.[1] In urban areas, access to public transportation may help residents overcome the difficulties posed by distance, but economic forces have driven grocery stores out of many cities in recent years, making them so few and far between that an individual's food shopping trip may require taking several buses or trains. In suburban and rural areas, public transportation is either very limited or unavailable, with supermarkets often many miles away from people's homes.

The other defining characteristic of food deserts is socio-economic: that is, they are most commonly found in black and brown communities and low-income areas (where many people don't have cars). Studies have found that wealthy districts have three times as many supermarkets as poor ones do,[2] that white neighborhoods contain an average of four times as many supermarkets as predominantly black ones do, and that grocery stores in African-American communities are usually smaller with less selection.[3] People's choices about what to eat are severely limited by the options available to them and what they can afford—and many food deserts contain an overabundance of fast food chains selling cheap "meat" and dairy-based foods that are high in fat, sugar and salt. Processed foods (such as snack cakes, chips and soda) typically sold by corner delis, convenience stores and liquor stores are usually just as unhealthy.

Food Empowerment Project's report, "Shining a Light on the Valley of Heart's Delight," shows that it is possible to overlook communities that are located in food deserts when relying on data collected by the US government. We found that, "Part of the problem is how the US government's North American Industry Classification System (NAICS is the standard used by the federal statistical agencies in classifying business establishments) categorizes retail outlets that sell food. According to the NAICS code, small corner grocery stores are statistically lumped together with supermarkets, such as Safeway, Whole Foods Market, etc. In other words, a community with no supermarket and two corner grocery stores that offer liquor and food would be counted as having two retail food outlets even though the food offered may be extremely limited and consist mainly of junk food."

In addition to this, we found that many of the convenience stores that had items such as a bunch of bananas or a few apples would sell the fruits individually. Because these items are not priced, the customers are often at the mercy of the person behind the counter who determines the cost then and there. Customers who don't have a good understanding of English might never ask the price of the item.

Those living in food deserts may also find it difficult to locate foods that are culturally appropriate for them, and dietary restrictions, such as lactose intolerance, gluten allergies, etc., also limit the food choices of those who do not have access to larger chain stores that have more selection. Additionally, studies have found that urban residents who purchase groceries at small neighborhood stores pay between 3 and 37 percent more than suburbanites buying the same products at supermarkets.[4]

Healthier foods are generally more expensive than unhealthful foods, particularly in food deserts. For instance, while the overall price of fruits and vegetables in the US increased by nearly 75 percent between 1989 and 2005, the price of fatty foods dropped by more than 26 percent during the same period.[5] While such inflation has strained the food budgets of many families regardless of their financial status, the higher cost of healthy foods often puts them entirely beyond the monetary means of many lower-income people.

Some cities have established farmers' markets in neighborhoods that are considered food deserts, giving residents access to affordable, fresh food.

While unhealthy eating may be economically cheaper in the short-term, the consequences of long-term constrained access to healthy foods is one of the main reasons that ethnic minority and low-income populations suffer from statistically higher rates of obesity, type 2 diabetes, cardiovascular disease, and other diet-related conditions than the general population.[6]

Whatever their age, obesity puts people at a greater risk for serious, even fatal health disorders (particularly coronary heart disease and diabetes,[7] the first and seventh leading causes of death in the US respectively):[8]

The incidence of diabetes among US adults doubled between 1996 and 2007, and "type 2 diabetes" (a variant of the disease that is often caused by obesity)[9] may account for 90 to 95 percent of these cases.[10] Only twenty years ago, type 2 diabetes was virtually unknown among people under 40 years old, but in the past decade it has increased tenfold among adolescents (mirroring this age group's escalating obesity rates).[11] While the incidence of type 2 diabetes has risen across demographic lines in recent years, the greatest increases have occurred among black and brown communities. The highest rates of escalation have been identified in Native American youth[12] and African-Americans and Latinos of all age groups, with these groups suffering disproportionately higher rates of type 2 diabetes compared to whites.[13] These are also the groups most likely to live in food deserts, and researchers have established a strong correlation between food insecurity and increased diabetes rates. One study of Chicago neighborhoods found the death rate from diabetes in food deserts to be twice that of areas offering access to grocery stores,[14] while another conducted in California found that adults ages 50 and over from black and brown communities had double the diabetes rate of whites from the same age demographic. Researchers explain this disparity by emphasizing that the high-calorie foods most readily available in food deserts put residents living in these areas at greater risk for diabetes in the first place, and that having restricted access to healthy foods also makes it harder for them to manage diabetes once they are diagnosed.[15]

Heart disease causes more than 2.4 million deaths in the US every year.[16] One of the main causes of cardiovascular disease is a diet high in unhealthy fats and low-density lipoprotein (LDL) cholesterol[17]—typified by the types of fare commonly available in food deserts. Just as African-Americans are statistically more likely than other populations to live in food deserts, heart disease kills more blacks every year than whites[18] (despite the fact that whites make up almost 80 percent of the total US populace, and blacks comprise slightly more than 13 percent).[19] Even children and adolescents living in food deserts are at greater risk for cardiovascular disease (both now and when they reach adulthood) due to the increased prevalence of obesity in those communities.[20]

Food for Thought

Public awareness of the formidable problems posed by food deserts is growing, thanks largely to the efforts of community activists,

> **FAST FACT**
> Urban residents who purchase groceries at small neighborhood stores pay more than people in the suburbs buying the same products at supermarkets.

entrepreneurs and government officials committed to increasing people's access to healthy food options. On the national level, First Lady Michelle Obama has spearheaded the "Let's Move" campaign to combat childhood obesity, which includes a goal of eradicating food deserts by 2017 with a $400 million investment from the government focused on providing tax breaks to supermarkets that open in food deserts.[21] Many urban areas are also implementing initiatives locally to solve their food desert challenges.

Chicago: More than 500,000 residents (mostly African-American) live in food deserts, and an additional 400,000 live in neighborhoods with a preponderance of fast food restaurants and no grocery stores nearby.[22] Some food justice activists have sought to close this gap by opening food co-ops in underserved areas where supermarkets have historically been unsuccessful. In addition to selling fresh and organic fruits and vegetables, bulk whole grains and beans, and soy-based meat substitutes, some of these stores (like Fresh Family Foods on the city's South Side) also offer cooking and nutrition classes to educate the public about making healthy food choices.[23]

Los Angeles: In 2008, the Los Angeles City Council voted to enact a moratorium on new fast food outlets in a 32-square-mile zone encompassing some of South L.A.'s most arid food deserts, an area where about 97 percent of the population is either Latino, African-American, or of mixed race.[24] Having fewer fast food restaurants created greater demand for more and better food choices, so Councilmembers subsequently passed another measure offering grocery stores and sit-down restaurants serving healthier meals financial incentives to open up in underserved communities.[25] These policies have so far succeeded in bringing the first new supermarket to South L.A. in about a decade.[26]

New York City: An estimated 750,000 New York City residents live in food deserts,[27] while about three million people live in places where stores that sell fresh produce are few or far away.[28] Supermarkets throughout New York City have closed down in recent years due to increasing rents and shrinking profit margins, but the disappearance of urban grocery stores has had the most serious impact on low-income communities, especially those that are predominantly African-American (such as East/Central Harlem and North/Central Brooklyn).[29] To fill this void, the city started its Green Carts program, which has been bringing affordable fresh fruits and vegetables to underserved areas while providing jobs for vendors since 2008. Hundreds of Green Carts are already on the streets in food deserts, and that number is rapidly increasing as prospective vendors obtain training, licenses and permits from the city.[30]

What Can I Do if I Live in a Food Desert?

If you recognize that you are living in a food desert, you can start by helping those in your community understand what this means and talk about ways to make change. Discussing different options, such as growing your own food, working with local retailers to sell healthy, vegan foods, etc., is a good place to start. It is also important to bring your ideas and concerns to policy makers—city councilmembers, state legislators, etc.

References

1. "Access to Affordable and Nutritious Food: Measuring and Understanding Food Deserts and Their Consequences." United States Department of Agriculture Economic Research Service. 2009. Retrieved 8/25/17 from https://www.ers.usda.gov/webdocs/publications/42711/12716_ap036_1_.pdf?v=41055

2. Walsh, Bryan. "It's Not Just Genetics." Time. June 12, 2008. http://www.time.com/time/magazine/article/0,9171,1813984,00.html (3/05/11)

3. Morland, K., Wing, S., et al. "Neighborhood characteristics associated with the location of food stores and food service places." American Journal of Preventive Medicine. January 2002, vol. 22(1): p. 23-29. http://www.ncbi.nlm.nih.gov/pubmed/11777675 (3/05/11)

4. Bullard, Robert D. (editor). Growing Smarter: Achieving Livable Communities, Environmental Justice, and Regional Equity. The MIT Press. 2007. p. 173. ttp://books.google.com/books?id=NAcmSchlTOYC&pg=PA173&lpg=PA173&dq=It+has+been+shown+that+... (3/05/11)

5. Walsh, Bryan. "It's Not Just Genetics." Time. June 12, 2008. http://www.time.com/time/magazine/article/0,9171,1813984,00.html (3/05/11)

6. Gallagher, Mari. "Examining the Impact of Food Deserts on Public Health in Chicago." Study commissioned by LaSalle Bank. 2006. http://www.marigallagher.com/2006/07/18/examining-the-impact-of-food-deserts-on-public-health-in-chicago-july-18-2006/ (8/21/17)

7. "NHANES data on the Prevalence of Overweight Among Children and Adolescents: United States, 2003–2006." CDC National Center for Health Statistics. 2010.http://www.cdc.gov/nchs/data/hestat/obesity_child_09_10/obesity_child_09_10.htm (3/05/11)

8. "Deaths and Mortality." Centers for Disease Control and Prevention. 2011. http://www.cdc.gov/nchs/fastats/deaths.htm (3/05/11)

9. "Type 2 diabetes: Causes." Mayo Clinic. 2011. http://www.mayoclinic.com/health/type-2-diabetes/DS00585/DSECTION=causes (3/05/11)

10. "National Diabetes Fact Sheet, 2011." Centers for Disease Control and Prevention. 2011. http://www.cdc.gov/diabetes/pubs/pdf/ndfs_2011.pdf (5/10/11)

11. Rates of new diagnosed cases of type 1 and type 2 diabetes on the rise among children, teens. (2017, April 17). Retrieved December 06, 2017, from https://www.nih.gov/news-events/news-releases/rates-new-diagnosed-cases-type-1-type-2-diabetes-rise-among-children-teens

12. Rates of new diagnosed cases of type 1 and type 2 diabetes on the rise among children, teens. (2017, April 17). Retrieved December 06, 2017, from https://www.nih.gov/news-events/news-releases/rates-new-diagnosed-cases-type-1-type-2-diabetes-rise-among-children-teens

13. "Diabetes Basics." American Diabetes Association. http://www.diabetes.org/diabetes-basics/type-2/ (3/05/11)

14. Curry, Andrew. "Bringing Healthy Fare to Big-City 'Food Deserts.'" Diabetes Forecast. December 2009. http://forecast.diabetes.org/magazine/your-ada/bringing-healthy-fare-big-city-food-deserts (4/17/11)

15. "The Inextricable Connection Between Food Insecurity and Diabetes." California Pan-Ethnic Health Network. May 2010. https://cpehn.org/sites/default/files/resource_files/diabetesbrief2010.pdf (9/5/17)

16. "Deaths and Mortality." Centers for Disease Control and Prevention. 2011. http://www.cdc.gov/nchs/fastats/deaths.htm (3/05/11)

17. "The Truth About Fats: The Good, the Bad, and the In-Between." Harvard Health Publications. 2015. Retrieved from https://www.health.harvard.edu/staying-healthy/the-truth-about-fats-bad-and-good (9/5/17)

18. "Heart Disease and African Americans." The Office of Minority Heatlh. 2010. https://minorityhealth.hhs.gov/omh/browse.aspx?lvl=4&lvlid=19 (3/05/11)

19. "QuickFacts: Population Estimates." US Census Bureau. July 1, 2016. https://www.census.gov/quickfacts/fact/table/US#viewtop (8/21/17)

20. "Childhood Obesity." Centers for Disease Control and Prevention. 2008. http://www.cdc.gov/healthyyouth/obesity/ (3/05/11)

21. "You All Took a Stand." White House Blog. February 20, 2010. http://www.whitehouse.gov/blog/2010/02/19/you-all-took-a-stand (4/02/11)

22. Gallagher, Mari. "Examining the Impact of Food Deserts on Public Health in Chicago." Study commissioned by LaSalle Bank. 2006. http://www.marigallagher.com/2006/07/18/examining-the-impact-of-food-deserts-on-public-health-in-chicago-july-18-2006/ (8/21/17)

23. Ogburn, Stephanie. "Would a Walmart solve West Oakland's and Nashville's food problems?" Grist. 5 Oct 2010. http://www.grist.org/article/food-2010-10-05-would-a-walmart-solve-oaklands-and-nashvilles-food-problems/PALL/print (4/02/11)

24. "Neighborhoods of the City of Los Angeles Population & Race 2010 Census." Los Angeles Almanac. 2010. http://www.laalmanac.com/population/po24la.htm (4/17/11)

25. Severson, Kim. "Los Angeles Stages a Fast Food Intervention." The New York Times. August 12, 2008. http://www.nytimes.com/2008/08/13/dining/13calo.html?scp=16&sq=food%20deserts&st=cse (4/02/11)

26. Medina, Jennifer. "In South Los Angeles, New Fast-Food Spots Get a 'No, Thanks.'" The New York Times. January 15, 2011. http://www.nytimes.com/2011/01/16/us/16fastfood.html?_r=1(4/02/11)

27. "Fresh Food for Urban Deserts." The New York Times. March 20, 2009. http://www.nytimes.com/2009/03/21/opinion/21sat4.html?scp=3&sq=food%20deserts&st=cse (4/02/11)

28. "Going to Market: New York City's Neighborhood Grocery Store and Supermarket Shortage." New York City Department of City Planning. 2008. http://www.nyc.gov/html/misc/pdf/going_to_market.pdf (8/21/17)

29. Gordon, C., Purciel-Hill, M., et al. "Measuring food deserts in New York City's low-income neighborhoods." Health Place. March 2011. Vol. 17(2), pages 696-700. http://www.ncbi.nlm.nih.gov/pubmed/21256070 (4/17/11)

30. McMahon, Jeff. "New York rolls veggie carts into food deserts; can other cities follow?" The New York Times. March 11, 2010. http://jeffmcmahon.com/2010/new-york-green-cart-chicago-farm-fork-financing/ (8/21/17)

EVALUATING THE AUTHOR'S ARGUMENTS:

Food Empowerment Project contends that urban food deserts contribute to chronic health problems, racial inequality, and poverty. Some cities are trying to bring healthy food options to food deserts. Do cities have a right to limit the number of fast-food restaurants in an area? Do they have a responsibility to bring in supermarkets? What factors should be considered?

Chapter 3

How Can We Ensure That People Have Food Security?

Community gardens provide nutritious produce to many inner city residents.

Viewpoint 1

Technology Can Meet the Demand

Ashley Hunter

"One of the main aims for food businesses will be how to achieve the balance of quality and quantity."

In the following viewpoint, Ashley Hunter discusses challenges arising from global population growth, which means a greater demand for food. The author argues that new technology will improve food production and reduce waste. Machines might replace some farm labor. Technology could identify quality versus flawed products and sort them accordingly. Doubling production in order to meet demand will be expensive, but possible, according to the author. Ashley Hunter works for TOMRA, a company that makes systems to minimize waste in the food, recycling, and mining industries.

AS YOU READ, CONSIDER THE FOLLOWING QUESTIONS:
1. According to the viewpoint, how fast is the global population growing?
2. What is likely to affect farm labor availability in many countries?
3. How can technology solve some problems with food production and distribution?

"The Effect of Population Growth on Efficiency in Food Production," by Ashley Hunter, TOMRA Sorting Food, August 23, 2016. Reprinted by permission.

The global population has been expanding rapidly for many years, standing at around 7.3 billion in 2016, due to a number of factors, such as advanced maternity and healthcare.

However, the rise brings with it a number of challenges around global sustainability, including the need for more food.

As an essential resource, the supply of food is a major concern across all countries, but—as with any resource—is dependent on growers, suppliers and distributors to bring it to market.

Exponential Growth

According to the Food and Agricultural Organization of the United Nations (FAO), the global population is expected to increase by around 2.3 billion people between now and 2050. Although this is a slower rate of growth than the one seen over the past 40 years, it is still a 30 per cent increase in the number of people who will need feeding.

At the same time, the amount of food that will need to be processed will rise by almost 70 per cent—and 100 per cent in the developing world—which will mean increased supply of several products to help cope with the demand.

Earnings in developing countries are expected to rise along with the growth and exceed so-called "economic poverty" levels, with the market demand for food continuing to grow in line with this.

Annual production of cereal will need to grow by almost one billion tons, and meat production by over 200 million tons, to a total of 470 million tons in 2050. 72 per cent of this will take place in developing countries, up from 58 per cent today.

Additional Factors

The Population Institute estimates that a 70 per cent increase in food production will also have to take into account increases in energy prices, as well as factors such as the groundwater depletion, the loss of farmland to urbanization, and potential flooding and droughts caused by climate change.

This rapid increase and the associated challenges will place additional strain on food production. The cost of doubling production in the developing world alone will require investment of almost $100

Technology and innovative solutions like seawater farming can help supply food to the world's population.

billion per year, not including any infrastructure that will be required to implement and support it.

A further problem will be increasing agricultural activity even though global governments are trying to reduce global greenhouse gas emissions—something the production and distribution of food has contributed to significantly in the past.

Multiple Challenges

A multi-targeted approach will be required to help overcome the many challenges. This will include looking at how new approaches to food production and changes to the supply chain can boost efficiency. The FAO believes there is potential to increase crop yields, with technology playing a major role in helping to boost production efficiency.

> **FAST FACT**
> In 1950, the world's population was about 2.5 billion. Today it is more than 7.7 billion. In 2050, it is expected to reach 9.7 billion.

The organization believes that having social and economic incentives in place will create more certainty over actual yield volumes and what is capable of being produced. Fears over a flattening out of yield volumes may be misplaced.

In addition to the size of the yield, boosting quality will also be a key aim for producers, as they try to improve processing capacity and availability. Meeting the needs of a rapidly expanding global population will require the production of food that meets safety standards.

The effect of urbanization must also be taken into account. A report from the Consultative Group for International Agricultural Research (CGIAR) suggests that rural-urban migration will continue to increase during the coming decades.

This growth will subsequently reduce farm labor availability in many countries and put pressure on supply chains. According to the CGIAR, this effect will require the development and use of technologies and production systems that increase input-use efficiency in agriculture.

Such approaches will contribute to global food and nutrition security while safeguarding the natural resource base and taking into account local, economic and social dynamics, as well as human and environmental health.

Balancing Quality and Quantity

As food safety standards rise and end-user tastes and demands change, quality will be a key issue. One of the main aims for food businesses will be how to achieve the balance of quality and quantity.

The investment needed to achieve these aims will also be a key subject for producers, particularly as the Population Institute says that meeting rising demand will come at a great cost.

Suppliers, distributors and concerns will all need to keep up to date with changes. This will mean ensuring food requirements are met, and that investment in future supply is adequate.

This investment extends to technology, which is playing a very important role in helping the industry to increase food production without compromising quality.

TOMRA's range of food sorting technology is designed to maximize yields and increase productivity while reducing waste, which boosts efficiency considerably. The sensor-based technology is capable of identifying imperfections and can help to increase the quality of the yield as well as the overall yield quantity, therefore minimizing waste.

Ideas and new technology have moved faster than population growth for centuries, helping to ensure people and business around the globe can keep up to speed with an ever-changing world.

New innovations will continue to maintain this balance by boosting food production and distribution efficiency in the years ahead.

EVALUATING THE AUTHOR'S ARGUMENTS:

Viewpoint author Ashley Hunter argues that technology can solve some of the problems with providing enough food to the global population. Do you think technology can solve some, most, or all of the problems? Does your trust in this viewpoint change knowing it's written by someone working for a company that builds this technology? Why or why not?

Viewpoint 2

Genetically Modified Food Can Eliminate World Hunger

Jennifer Ackerman

"Genetic engineering can help address the urgent problems of food shortage and hunger."

In the following excerpted viewpoint, Jennifer Ackerman explores debates about GM foods, including claims that the problem with GM foods is not human health but the environment. Each GM organism needs to be individually evaluated, but that's not happening. Still, some experts argue that GM foods have great value in eliminating world hunger and keeping people healthier. It's a matter of balancing the needs of farmers, profits for companies, and the safety of nature. Jennifer Ackerman is an award-winning science writer whose work has appeared in *Scientific American* and the *New York Times*.

AS YOU READ, CONSIDER THE FOLLOWING QUESTIONS:
1. What advantage do genetically engineered crops have over pesticides?
2. How do genes flow between food crops and unwanted weeds?
3. Why are genetically engineered seeds often unavailable to farmers in the developing world?

"Food: How Altered?" by Jennifer Ackerman, National Geographic Partners, LLC. Reprinted by permission.

Just what are genetically engineered foods, and who is eating them? What do we know about their benefits—and their risks? What effect might engineered plants have on the environment and on agricultural practices around the world? Can they help feed and preserve the health of the Earth's burgeoning population?

[...]

Can Biotech Foods Harm the Environment?

Most scientists agree: The main safety issues of genetically engineered crops involve not people but the environment. "We've let the cat out of the bag before we have real data, and there's no calling it back," says Allison Snow, a plant ecologist at Ohio State University.

Snow is known for her research on "gene flow," the movement of genes via pollen and seeds from one population of plants to another, and she and some other environmental scientists worry that genetically engineered crops are being developed too quickly and released on millions of acres of farmland before they've been adequately tested for their possible long-term ecological impact.

Advocates of genetically engineered crops argue that the plants offer an environmentally friendly alternative to pesticides, which tend to pollute surface and groundwater and harm wildlife. The use of Bt varieties has dramatically reduced the amount of pesticide applied to cotton crops. But the effects of genetic engineering on pesticide use with more widely grown crops are less clear-cut.

What might be the effect of these engineered plants on so-called nontarget organisms, the creatures that visit them? Concerns that crops with built-in insecticides might damage wildlife were inflamed in 1999 by the report of a study suggesting that Bt corn pollen harmed monarch butterfly caterpillars.

Monarch caterpillars don't feed on corn pollen, but they do feed on the leaves of milkweed plants, which often grow in and around cornfields. Entomologists at Cornell University showed that in the laboratory Bt corn pollen dusted onto milkweed leaves stunted or killed some of the monarch caterpillars that ate the leaves. For some environmental activists this was confirmation that genetically engineered crops were dangerous to wildlife. But follow-up studies in the field, reported last fall, indicate that pollen densities from Bt corn rarely reach damaging levels on milkweed, even when monarchs are feeding on plants within a cornfield.

"The chances of a caterpillar finding Bt pollen doses as high as those in the Cornell study are negligible," says Rick Hellmich, an entomologist with the Agricultural Research Service and one author of the follow-up report. "Butterflies are safer in a Bt cornfield than they are in a conventional cornfield, when they're subjected to chemical pesticides that kill not just caterpillars but most insects in the field."

Perhaps a bigger concern has to do with insect evolution. Crops that continuously make Bt may hasten the evolution of insects impervious to the pesticide. Such a breed of insect, by becoming resistant to Bt, would rob many farmers of one of their safest, most environmentally friendly tools for fighting the pests.

To delay the evolution of resistant insects, US government regulators, working with biotech companies, have devised special measures for farmers who grow Bt crops. Farmers must plant a moat or "refuge" of conventional crops near their engineered crops. The idea is to prevent two resistant bugs from mating. The few insects that emerge from Bt fields resistant to the insecticide would mate with their nonresistant neighbors living on conventional crops nearby; the result could be offspring susceptible to Bt. The theory is that if growers follow requirements, it will take longer for insects to develop resistance.

It was difficult initially to convince farmers who had struggled to keep European corn borers off their crops to let the insects live and eat part of their acreage to combat resistance. But a 2001 survey by major agricultural biotech companies found that almost 90 percent of US farmers complied with the requirements.

Many ecologists believe that the most damaging environmental impact of biotech crops may be gene flow. Could transgenes that confer resistance to insects, disease, or harsh growing conditions give weeds a competitive advantage, allowing them to grow rampantly?

"Genes flow from crops to weeds all the time when pollen is transported by wind, bees, and other pollinators," says Allison Snow. "There's no doubt that transgenes will jump from engineered crops into nearby relatives." But since gene flow usually takes place only between closely related species, and since most major US crops don't have close relatives growing nearby, it's extremely unlikely that gene flow will occur to create problem weeds.

Still, Snow says, "even a very low probability event could occur when you're talking about thousands of acres planted with food crops." And in developing countries, where staple crops are more frequently planted near wild relatives, the risk of transgenes escaping is higher. While no known superweeds have yet emerged, Snow thinks it may just be a matter of time.

Given the risks, many ecologists believe that industry should step up the extent and rigor of its testing and governments should strengthen their regulatory regimes to more fully address environmental effects. "Every transgenic organism brings with it a different set of potential risks and benefits," says Snow. "Each needs to be evaluated on a case-by-case basis. But right now only one percent of USDA biotech research money goes to risk assessment."

Can Biotech Foods Help Feed the World?

"Eight hundred million people on this planet are malnourished," says Channapatna Prakash, a native of India and an agricultural scientist at the Center for Plant Biotechnology Research at Tuskegee University, "and the number continues to grow."

Genetic engineering can help address the urgent problems of food shortage and hunger, say Prakash and many other scientists. It can increase crop yields, offer crop varieties that resist pests and disease, and provide ways to grow crops on land that would otherwise not support farming because of drought conditions, depleted soils, or soils plagued by excess salt or high levels of aluminum and iron. "This technology is extremely versatile," Prakash explains, "and it's easy for farmers to use because it's built into the seed. The farmers just plant the seeds, and the seeds bring new features in the plants."

Some critics of genetic engineering argue that the solution to hunger and malnutrition lies in redistributing existing food supplies. Others believe that the ownership by big multinational companies of key biotechnology methods and genetic information is crippling public-sector efforts to use this technology to address the needs of subsistence farmers. The large companies that dominate the industry,

While genetically modified foods have their critics, supporters believe they are a solution for feeding a hungry world.

critics also note, are not devoting significant resources to developing seed technology for subsistence farmers because the investment offers minimal returns. And by patenting key methods and materials, these companies are stifling the free exchange of seeds and techniques vital to public agricultural research programs, which are already under severe financial constraints. All of this bodes ill, say critics, for farmers in the developing world.

Prakash agrees that there's enough food in the world. "But redistribution is just not going to happen," he says. "The protest against biotech on political grounds is a straw man for a larger frustration with globalization, a fear of the power of large multinational corporations. People say that this technology is just earning profit for big companies. This is true to some extent, but the knowledge that companies have developed in the production of profitable crops can easily be transferred and applied to help developing nations."

"Biotechnology is no panacea for world hunger," says Prakash, "but it's a vital tool in a toolbox, one that includes soil and water conservation, pest management, and other methods of sustainable agriculture, as well as new technologies."

The debate over the use of biotechnology in developing countries recently went from simmer to boil about rice, which is eaten by three billion people and grown on hundreds of millions of small farms.

"White rice," explains Dean DellaPenna, "is low in protein. It has very little iron, and virtually no vitamin A." However, in 1999 a team of scientists led by Ingo Potrykus, of the Swiss Federal Institute of Technology, and Peter Beyer, of the University of Freiburg, Germany, announced a new breakthrough: They had introduced into rice plants two daffodil genes and one bacterial gene that enable the rice to produce in its grains beta-carotene, a building block of vitamin A. According to the World Health Organization, between 100 million and 140 million children in the world suffer from vitamin A deficiency, some 500,000 go blind every year because of that deficiency, and half of those children die within a year of losing their sight. "Golden rice," so named for the yellow color furnished by the beta-carotene, was hailed by some as a potential solution to the suffering and illness caused by vitamin A deficiency.

Skeptics consider golden rice little more than a public relations ploy by the biotechnology industry, which they say exaggerated its benefits. "Golden rice alone won't greatly diminish vitamin A deficiency," says Marion Nestle. "Beta-carotene, which is already widely available in fruit and vegetables, isn't converted to vitamin A when people are malnourished. Golden rice does not contain much beta-carotene, and whether it will improve vitamin A levels remains to be seen."

Potrykus and Beyer are now developing new versions of the rice that may be more effective in delivering

FAST FACT
Today, nearly 93 percent of soybeans and 88 percent of corn crops grown in the US are genetically modified, according to the FDA.

beta-carotene for the body to convert to vitamin A. Their plan is to put the improved rices free of charge into the hands of poor farmers. According to Beyer, golden rice is still at least four years away from distribution. It could take much longer if opposing groups delay plans for field trials and safety studies.

What Next?

Whether biotech foods will deliver on their promise of eliminating world hunger and bettering the lives of all remains to be seen. Their potential is enormous, yet they carry risks—and we may pay for accidents or errors in judgment in ways we cannot yet imagine. But the biggest mistake of all would be to blindly reject or endorse this new technology. If we analyze carefully how, where, and why we introduce genetically altered products, and if we test them thoroughly and judge them wisely, we can weigh their risks against their benefits to those who need them most.

EVALUATING THE AUTHOR'S ARGUMENTS:

Viewpoint author Jennifer Ackerman discusses the pros and cons of GM crops. Do you agree with the conclusions that use of GM foods may be necessary to feed the world? Why or why not? What further research might clarify or change your opinion?

Viewpoint 3

Food Security Is Land Security

Michael Igoe Devex

In the following viewpoint, Michael Igoe Devex discusses how land ownership and use might change to increase food production. Small-scale farming supports rural communities throughout the world. However, these farmers sometimes lose their land to large companies. Big agricultural businesses can boost efficiency and productivity, but they don't always support local communities. Balancing the two groups is tricky but necessary for future food production. Michael Igoe Devex is a journalist who covers US foreign aid, global health, climate change, and development finance.

"Land remains a fundamental component of the world's ability to feed itself."

AS YOU READ, CONSIDER THE FOLLOWING QUESTIONS:

1. How many people worldwide work in agriculture?
2. How do people treat their land when they are confident they will keep it?
3. How can short-term gain harm long-term success in food production and the economy?

"Food Security Is Land Security," by Michael Igoe Devex, July 11, 2014. Reprinted by permission.

How can the world feed a global population of 9 billion by 2050? The answer might seem simple enough: grow more food.

The "green revolution," a period of agricultural modernization efforts that bolstered food production and staved off famines in the mid-20th century, showed how a concerted global effort can invigorate and expand food systems with technology transfers and new techniques when farmers find the tools at their disposal to invest in more productive practices.

With concerns mounting over food price shocks, rapid population growth, changing consumption patterns and climate change impacts, calls for a "second green revolution" have grown almost cliché. And when those calls fail to engage with the very real tradeoffs that will be required if the world's food production capacity is going to reach—and sustain—even greater heights, they risk sounding naïve.

Land is at the center of those challenges and tradeoffs. While the nature of the relationship between people and the planet has changed in once unthinkable ways, land remains a fundamental component of the world's ability to feed itself.

"I can't think of another sector that is so tied to the land. Land is the chief, primary input in all agricultural production," said Nate Kline, chief of party for the Enabling Agricultural Trade project at Fintrac.

But the demands the global population is placing on land resources are changing, and so are the ways that people think about the most effective ways to organize land ownership and use.

More people live in urban areas than rural areas for the first time in human history. Cities must be linked to food production and distribution chains that are capable of supplying nutrition to large numbers of people at a consistent and dependable rate—and from a distance. That must all happen at a time when climate change is expected to introduce unpredictable shocks and when more of the global population is demanding higher-input foods like meat and dairy.

Against that backdrop, the way families, communities, nations, and international organizations choose to organize land and secure the relative strength of some land rights and land ownership claims over others will be central to answering tough questions about a food-secure future.

How can we produce more food, and at what cost? How do we feed a growing population while still upholding the rights of existing land-holders to benefit from the use and development of their resources? Who should decide what constitutes a right to use and develop land in the first place? Our answers to these questions will help to determine the future of human life on Earth.

For Farmers, Food Security Is a Healthy Income

The "only way" we're going to achieve food security for large numbers of people, said Olaf Kula, program manager for ACDI/VOCA's West Africa regional office, is to produce a lot more food in the countries that are food-insecure.

But achieving food security is not just about whether the world can grow enough food. It is also about how the agricultural sector, which employs more than 1 billion people, can become a more viable, dependable source of income for people living in rural areas. The income of the very poor is more closely linked to growth in the agricultural sector than to growth in any other sector, according to research from the US Agency for International Development's land tenure division.

When land users feel secure that their land will belong to them as long as they wish to keep it, that it will not be arbitrarily seized by foreign investors, by other land-using groups, or forced out of agricultural use by encroaching development, then those individuals are more likely to invest in the long-term development and stewardship of their land and resources.

With that kind of security often come better land-use choices—to conserve water and soil nutrients, for example, instead of exhausting them for short-term gain. And it can mean landholders are more willing to shoulder the upfront costs of fertilizers, seed varieties and equipment that can lead to higher incomes and more marketable crops over time. When families sell more and better food, not only do they have more nutritious yields, but those yields generate more income to spend on household food needs.

Land grabbing introduces a lack of food security for agricultural communities, as in the case of Kenyan land siezed by British colonists for use as tea plantations in the 1900s.

"There is a direct link between the security that a person has, or at least the perceived security that they feel in their access to the land and their willingness … to undertake investments that over time may pay off … but that take more than one growing season to pay for themselves," Kline said.

With more money from marketable crops, families have the option to invest in their own nutrition—and to reinvest in the enhanced long-term productivity of their land and resources by buying better inputs and equipment and accessing better management techniques.

The Right Kinds of Investment

A world that grows more food but does so without enhancing the profitability of small-scale farming will not be food-secure as long as small-scale farming remains the backbone of rural economies throughout the developing world.

But by the same token, the relationship between people and land has shifted too dramatically to imagine that large-scale investment and production won't be a big part of any global food security solution. As demand for land and food grows—driven by concerns over food shortages and demand for non-food commodities like biofuels—the incentive to buy and sell large tracts of land continues to increase.

Many parts of the world, but perhaps most notoriously Africa, have witnessed a rise in large-scale, commercial, foreign investment in tracts of land measuring in the hundreds of thousands of hectares—what many refer to derisively (and sometimes misleadingly) as "land-grabbing."

"You can't find 100,000 hectares that don't have people on it anywhere in Africa, unless it's on water," Kula said.

Transferring the rights and responsibilities for food production from smallholder farmers to larger agribusinesses can boost efficiency and productivity. Large producers enjoy economies of scale, and they are able to establish relationships with commercial buyers that benefit from the consistency and dependability of large-scale production.

The challenge, Kula said, is to find opportunities within large-scale investment plans for smallholder farmers to boost their productivity—or to benefit from the sale of their land if they choose to divest. That means finding good models for responsible, fair and socially inclusive development; those models must either draw smallholders into investment schemes or compensate them fairly for the land they choose to give up.

"Some of these arrangements work better than others," Kula said.

But for either of them to happen, smallholder farmers must be able to demonstrate their legitimate claim to a parcel of land.

A Strong Role for Public Action

In order for that pro-poor sentiment to become a reality, smallholders' rights to own and transfer land must be secured so that they can either be officially incorporated into agricultural development schemes or afforded the opportunity to profit from the sale of their property. That security demands a strong role for government action,

> **FAST FACT**
> By the end of this century, population growth may slow dramatically. The population may flatten out at around 10.9 billion, according to data from the United Nations.

and a willingness among public officials to resist tempting opportunities for short-term gain in favor of a more regulated, inclusive development process.

In Liberia, according to Kula, that has often not been the case. Some foreign companies have signed agreements with the government for "very long-term leases on huge tracts of land" with the understanding that those lease agreements will help to reduce poverty and increase food security.

"A number of these companies have not fulfilled their commitments to the socially inclusive part or the equitable and transparent displacement of smallholders," Kula said.

But while private investors have a responsibility to uphold their commitments, so do governments have a responsibility to monitor and enforce them.

"The government, in the case of Liberia, has not established the rules clearly and the enforcement mechanism and the consequences for failing to honor these arrangements," Kula suggested.

Government officials involved in land lease arrangements face a choice: facilitate the deal and take a large fee from the foreign investor, or take time and spend political capital to establish a robust rules framework for compensating smallholder farmers and then spend years monitoring and policing that rules framework. Too often, governments choose short-term gain over long-term benefit.

"The incentives for land-grabbing are multiple," Kula said.

There are some encouraging signs. In April, beverage giant PepsiCo joined Coca-Cola on the list of companies that now agree to uphold the Food and Agriculture Organization's Voluntary Guidelines on the Responsible Governance of Tenure, which seek to promote food security and other goals by upholding local land access and ownership rights.

But in a sector as complex and context-specific as land tenure and property rights, even those success stories raise challenging questions that the international community has to confront as it moves forward on fortifying the link between land rights and food security.

Avoiding the "Clash" of the Formal and Informal

Customary land ownership systems still apply in many parts of the world, and in many cases have existed for so long partly because they have not faced significant outside threats or shocks.

"When you have relative land abundance, customary tenure systems can function quite well. Where you begin to see competition for the land, where you begin to see demand for larger tracts of land by larger and larger scale investors, … there begins to be this sort of clash," Kline said.

With more efforts underway to formalize customary land use rights into officially recognized laws, international organizations and governments are finding they must strike a careful balance between promoting universal principles—like FAO's voluntary guidelines—and adhering to local customs and norms.

In Papua New Guinea, for example, 93 percent of the country's land is held in customary titles, arranged according to various rules by the roughly 800 different tribes who live there. Some of those systems are patrilineal, some are matrilineal, with significant variation between them. The government is now seeking to survey those customary rights and codify them into laws that can be defended and upheld in courts and against external pressure.

"Rather than creating formal requirement for equal treatment for men and women, … the government of Papua New Guinea is leaving it up to the communities themselves to establish their own articles of incorporation," Kline said.

That approach might satisfy proponents of upholding local cultures and local land use traditions, but it does less to forward international best practices and guidelines around land governance.

"What you're beginning to see in Papua New Guinea is they're creating … in perpetuity a limitation on most women's rights to actually vote on the decisions about how land is used," Kline said, adding: "It seems that the jury is really still out on the benefits that greater tenure security have on women."

The Way Forward

Research on the link between land tenure and food security is growing but, as Jack Keefe said, "It's still an evolving field and there's no one answer."

"I think the more that you're bringing people around the table, sharing ideas, and then trying to have evidence-based research in place, ... that's really the way forward," said Keefe, an associate for land and market development at Tetra Tech, working on a pastoral resiliency project in Ethiopia to secure lands held in common by pastoral groups.

Formalizing customary land rights and ensuring that smallholders' claims are officially registered can help advance sustainable agriculture. But those efforts must be based on inclusive planning and informed by a public discussion about how to produce the food that we need with the land that we have.

EVALUATING THE AUTHOR'S ARGUMENTS:

Viewpoint author Michael Igoe Devex discusses an often overlooked aspect of food security: land ownership. Who should determine who owns land? What responsibility does the government have? What responsibility do large international businesses have?

Viewpoint 4

Eat Plants, Not Animals

Dana Ellis Hunnes

"Pound-for-pound, gallon-for-gallon, animal-sourced foods use vastly more water and carbon to produce than plant-based foods."

In the following viewpoint, Dana Ellis Hunnes makes the argument for switching from an animal-based diet to a plant-based diet. The author notes that plant food crops use far less water than do animal foods. Plant food crops also produce fewer polluting greenhouse gases. Hunnes suggests that people eliminate meat and animal products from their diet at least some of the time, if not all of the time, in order to help the planet and to feed more people. Dana Ellis Hunnes is a dietitian and professor in UCLA's Department of Community Health Sciences.

AS YOU READ, CONSIDER THE FOLLOWING QUESTIONS:
1. How much water is used to produce animal-based foods?
2. How else do animal products affect the environment?
3. Can people get enough protein from a plant-based diet?

"The Case for Plant Based," by Dana Ellis Hunnes, PhD, MPH, RD, Adjunct Assistant Professor, UCLA Fielding School of Public Health and Senior Dietitian at UCLA Health. (Written for the UCLA Sustainability Committee website.) Reprinted by permission.

Eating a plant-based diet is not just good for our health; it is good for Earth's health. In fact, "Shifting away from animal-based foods [could not only] add up to 49% to the global food supply without expanding croplands," but would also significantly reduce carbon emissions and waste byproducts that end up in our oceans and as seafood byproducts (Jalava et al, 2014).

If each and every person in the United States gave up meat and dairy products on one or more days of the week, ideally, all days of the week, we would save the environment from thousands of tons of carbon emissions. In fact, in one year, animal husbandry creates as much carbon emissions as the entire transportation sector.

Similarly, by reducing our animal-based foods consumption, we would reduce our water use at least by half as animal husbandry utilizes more than 50% of fresh water.

These reductions would reduce the direct and indirect threats to Earth's health and habitability for us, and for all wildlife, flora, and fauna.

As for nutritional concerns: Pound-for-pound, gallon-for-gallon, animal-sourced foods use vastly more water and carbon to produce than plant-based foods. However, ounce-for-ounce, the amount of protein that you get from plant-sources, such as legumes, seeds, and grains, is closely on par, plus full of other healthful nutrients including fiber, sterols, stanols, and vitamins and minerals.

To put this into context:
- 1 pound of beef requires anywhere between 2,000 and 8,000 gallons of water to produce, according to studies conducted by UC Davis. Much of this water is used in creating the feed for the cows, whether it is grass or grain (Beckett & Oltjen, 1993).
- Similarly, 1 gallon of cow's milk requires 1950 gallons of water.
- Conversely, 1 pound of Tofu requires 302 gallons of water to produce, and it requires 290 gallons of water to produce 1 pound of unprocessed oats.

Now, for those of you worried about protein content:

Food	Protein	Cost
Beef	90–100 grams protein	20–80 gallons of water per gram protein
Milk	128 grams protein	15 gallons of water per gram protein
Tofu	45–55 grams protein	6 gallons of water per gram protein
Oats	75 grams protein	3.8 gallons of water per gram protein

From a water perspective, using simple mathematics, it is much more efficient and cost-effective to eat plant foods than animal foods. From a greenhouse gas emissions perspective, it is without doubt; it is significantly better for the environment to eat plant-based foods.

If we all eliminated meat and milk from our diets and went to plant sources of these foods, we would be saving at least 50% of our water use. We would be saving untouched habitats (rainforests, marshes) from being destroyed to produce more livestock feed, and we would be creating less pollution in our waterways, streams, and oceans that indirectly threaten human, animal, and plant lives.

What Are Some Ways We Can Eat Plant-Based on UCLA's Campus?

There are many places throughout campus you can purchase plant-based meals. Plant-based items are available at all eating outlets, from the hospital, to the residence halls, to the food courts; it is possible to find something to suit your tastes.

Medical Center: The medical center (Westwood and Santa Monica) offers Meatless Monday all year round where special hot-entrée vegetarian and vegan items are available in addition to the salad bars, which offer an array of vegetables and mixed vegetarian/vegan dressed salads.

> **FAST FACT**
> Polls suggest that 3 to 7% of Americans are vegetarian. About 1 to 3% eat a strictly vegan diet with no animal products. Both diets are more common among young people.

Cafeterias in college dining halls and other institutions are moving toward greater plant-based offerings.

In addition to Meatless Monday, every day you can find several vegetarian and vegan items available at the deli, grille, and international corner. New offerings are always being created seasonally as well. In fact, the hospital has recently added new recipes that contain whole grains, seeds, and legumes including bulgur and faro dishes along with quinoa and lentils.

Campus: Throughout campus you can find multiple vegetarian and vegan items as well!

Beefless Thursdays are offered at the main dining halls throughout campus to highlight the negative environmental impacts associated with beef production. "Green Mondays" is a new educational campaign on campus, demonstrating the impacts of animal agriculture on the environment, from water use to greenhouse gas emissions.

Additionally, getting a meatless option on The Hill is easy! Every platform station at every dining hall offers vegetarian options for every meal, including vegan quesadillas at Rendezvous; lentil, beet, wheat, berry, and kale bowls at Bruin Plate; and ginger-tofu stir fries at Feast, to name a few.

The great thing about UCLA is that we are making it easier for you and U to find the healthy foods that support the mission of UCLA sustainability, Zero Waste by 2020 and 20% sustainable food purchases by 2020. Additionally, UCLA offers sustainable service-ware, composting, recycling, and opportunities to improve both UCLA's water and carbon footprint, as well as your own.

References

Jalava M, Kummu M, Porkka M, Siebert S, and Varis O (2014). Diet Change–a solution to reduce water use? Environ. Res. lett. 9(7):1-14.

Beckett, J. L., and J. W. Oltjen (1993). Estimation of the water requirement for beef production in the United States. J. Anim. Sci. 71: 818-826.

United Nations (2016). "First Global Integrated Marine Assessment (First World Ocean Assessment). Oceans and Law of the Sea, an Integrated Report. http://www.un.org/depts/los/global_reporting/WOA_RegProcess.htm.

EVALUATING THE AUTHOR'S ARGUMENTS:

In this viewpoint, author Dana Ellis Hunnes maintains that people should give up (or at least reduce) meat and animal products in favor of a plant-based diet. Did her argument convince you? Why or why not? Why might people avoid switching to a vegetarian or vegan diet?

Viewpoint 5

Let's Eat Insects

Rick LeBlanc

"The notion of insects as food might make your skin crawl, but they have been a common part of the human diet for thousands of years."

In the following viewpoint, Rick LeBlanc explores the possibility of using insects as a sustainable food. Insects are nutritious and can provide dietary protein. They are less harmful to the environment than other animal meat sources. Companies around the world are starting insect farming businesses. In some countries, insects are already a familiar food. In the United States, producers will have an uphill battle convincing Americans to give them a try. Rick LeBlanc is a writer who covers sustainability topics.

AS YOU READ, CONSIDER THE FOLLOWING QUESTIONS:
1. How common is the eating of insects?
2. What are advantages to eating insects?
3. What challenges will producers have to overcome to convince people to eat insects?

"Edible Insects as a Sustainable Food Alternative," by Rick LeBlanc, Dotdash publishing family, October 14, 2019. Reprinted by permission.

No matter how unpalatable insects might seem to you, creepy crawlies such as silkworms, caterpillars, and crickets just might be a key source of protein in your food. They also might be an important way to increase sustainability in the food chain.

The notion of insects as food might make your skin crawl, but they have been a common part of the human diet for thousands of years. Today, they are actively consumed in various parts of the world. The farming of insects such as crickets has taken off in many countries including Thailand, India, South Africa, and Kenya.

There are various estimates about how widespread insect-eating is. Many proponents of entomophagy (the technical term for eating insects) claim that insects are eaten in 80% of countries, while the Food and Agriculture Organization (FAO) of the United Nations said in a 2013 report that 20% of the world's population eats insects. Here's a closer look at the potential for insects as sustainable food alternatives.

Why Eat Insects?

Insects are cheap, nutritious, and—according to some supporters—delicious. There are over 2,100 edible insect species, which offers a vast array of options for food dishes. FAO states that edible insects contain high-quality protein, amino acids, vitamins, calcium, zinc, and iron for humans.

When you have a healthy source of protein, minerals, and other important nutrients, a Michelin restaurant taste experience might arguably be a secondary priority. Consider that 100 grams of beef contain 29 grams of protein, but also 21 grams of fat. On the other hand, 100 grams of grasshopper contain 20 grams of protein and only 6 grams of fat.

In addition to nutritional value, commercial insect production has a much smaller negative impact on the environment than traditional sources of protein. Rearing conventional livestock, for example, accounts for a staggering 18% of total greenhouse gas emissions. But insect breeding releases much less greenhouse gas, methane, and ammonia than raising cattle and pigs, and requires less water.

While a plate of fried grasshoppers might turn the stomachs of many Americans, insects are regularly consumed in many countries around the world.

History of Insect Consumption

As mentioned above, insects have been consumed by humans for thousands of years, starting from the time of ancient hunters and gatherers. The practice continued to evolve with succeeding civilizations. The Greeks and Romans were known to dine on locusts and beetle larvae. One renowned Greek philosopher and scientist even wrote about harvesting tasty cicadas. The New Testament describes how St. John the Baptist survived on honey and locusts when he lived in the deep desert. The ancient Algerians ate locusts as a cheap and nutritious source of food after boiling them in salt water and drying them in the sun. Australian aboriginals would eat foods made of moths, witchetty grubs, and honeypot ants.

What Countries Eat Insects the Most?

Mexico, Brazil, Ghana, Thailand, China, and the Netherlands are some of the countries where insect-eating is most widely practiced today.

Arguably, Mexico is the country where bug consumption is most popular. You will find many Mexican delicacies such as candy-covered worms, chocolate-covered locusts, and ant eggs soaked in butter.

Farther south, Brazilians like to collect ants, remove wings, fry, and eat them. They also like ants dipped in chocolate. To them, ants simply taste like mint. Bug-eating has had a long tradition in many parts of that country.

Surprisingly, insects account for up to 60% of the dietary protein in a rural African diet. Termites are very popular, especially in Ghana. How about snack food? Crickets, grasshoppers, and many varieties of worms fill this role in Thailand. Many Thailand bars also serve fried bugs along with their libations. In China, fried silkworm moth larvae and roasted bee larvae are two common items in food stalls.

Eating Bugs in the United States

With the US edible insect industry already registering $20 million annually in sales, there seems to be an opportunity for growth. While not yet widely popular, many food makers are convincing Americans to eat bugs by educating them about the various health and environmental benefits associated with the practice.

Silkworm soup and grasshopper tacos are available in some San Francisco, New York, and Washington, D.C., restaurants. Recently, Exo, a cricket protein bar, raised more than $4 million from big-name investors. The major insect-based food makers like Exo, Chirap, and Chapul all note on their packaging that their products are gluten-free. Exo and Chapul even specify that their products contain no dairy or soy. Some followers of the Paleo diet in America are already eating cricket powder protein bars.

Protein is also a priority for CrossFit devotees and weightlifters, and companies like Exo are finding support from such people.

Sustainability

According to a recent study from the University of Copenhagen, insects are an extremely sustainable source of protein, much more so than meat. And according to the U.N., the worldwide livestock industry accounts for over 14.5% of global greenhouse gas emissions. By comparison, cricket production is 20 times more efficient as a protein source than cattle, and it produces 80 times less methane. Additionally, insects can thrive on organic waste, allowing farmers

> **FAST FACT**
> According to the U.N., the worldwide livestock industry accounts for over 14.5% of global greenhouse gas emissions. Cricket production produces much less pollution.

to cut back on growing the grain used in animal feed, which requires significant energy and water resources.

The rearing of insects requires dramatically less food than raising beef. For example, according to the FAO, insects consume just 2 pounds of feed to produce 1 pound of meat, while cattle require 8 pounds of feed to generate 1 pound of beef. That's why the U.N. called for swapping burgers for bugs.

Insect farming makes economic sense as well. As insects are cold-blooded, they require less energy to stay warm. This helps explain why they are more efficient at converting feed into protein. Consider that crickets need four times less feed than sheep, 12 times less than cattle, and half as much as broiler chickens and pigs to produce the same amount of protein.

While many people are still aghast at the thought of eating bugs, insects are increasingly recognized as a good protein alternative for the future. Current projections say that, by 2050, the world's population will reach 9 billion by 2050. The urgency for sustainable food protein alternatives such as those provided by entomophagy will only continue to grow.

Opportunities and Challenges

Sustainability, increasing demand for protein, and low feed-to-protein ratios are some of the reasons startups around the world are keen on establishing insect farming businesses. Ynsect, an insect farming company from France, has raised over $160 million since is started in 2011. AgriProtein, a startup from South Africa, has raised more than $105 million in funding so far.

But the industry is not without its share of challenges. The dislike, disgust, or fear of much of the populace toward eating insects will require a major shift in public perception. Given the resistance in the marketplace, a potential entrepreneur must deal with operational aspects of starting a bug production operation while also trying to educate consumers about the benefits of insect-based food and convince them to try it.

Conclusion

While insects are a sustainable, alternative protein source for the future, it will take time to develop a culture where people feel as comfortable eating insects as other foods. Maybe large-scale production and mass acceptance of insect-eating in other parts of the world—or by some groups in the US—can help insect-based food to become gradually accepted as an everyday protein source for the masses.

There will be a great interest and a sense of urgency to see how the new insect-farming companies perform over the next couple of decades. Perhaps there will be a point of convergence for a growing and increasingly sophisticated industry and a gradually transforming consumer palate.

EVALUATING THE AUTHOR'S ARGUMENTS:

Viewpoint author Rick LeBlanc suggests that eating insects is a way to feed people in the future. Do you think insects will become a common part of the American diet? Why or why not? Has the author convinced you that eating insects might not be as bad as you might think?

Facts About Food Security

Editor's note: These facts can be used in reports to add credibility when making important points or claims.

Food security means having enough food. In addition, the food should be healthy and tasty. It should also be culturally appropriate. This means the people buying or receiving the food are familiar with it, know how to prepare it, and can read any labels or instructions.

The US Department of Agriculture (USDA) uses the following labels and definitions:

High food security: no reported indications of food-access problems or limitations.

Marginal food security: one or two reported indications—typically of anxiety over food sufficiency or shortage of food in the house. Little or no indication of changes in diets or food intake.

Low food security: reports of reduced quality, variety, or desirability of diet. Little or no indication of reduced food intake. (Food insecurity without hunger.)

Very low food security: reports of multiple indications of disrupted eating patterns and reduced food intake. (Food insecurity with hunger.)

Food Insecurity Worldwide

According to the World Health Organization, over 2 billion people suffer from moderate to severe food insecurity. That means they do not have regular access to safe, nutritious, and sufficient food. That's over 26% of the population, as of 2018, when the last study was done. The chances of being food insecure are higher for women than men.

In 2018, an estimated 821.6 million people did not have enough to eat, according to the World Health Organization. That's one in nine people. Hunger is most common in Africa.

Even when people have enough food, they may suffer from nutritional deficiencies. The largest number of undernourished people live in Asia: more than 500 million of them. Poor nutrition is responsible for 45 percent of child deaths in low- and middle-income countries. It also leads to stunted growth and poor brain development in millions of children.

The Global Hunger Index (GHI) is a measure that combines four indicators: undernourishment, child wasting, child stunting, and child mortality. GHI has been falling in most countries, even those with high population growth.

Factors threatening global food security include: rising prices, drought and other climate disasters, arable land shortages, and increasing demand. Factors contributing to hunger and food insecurity include: violence, poor access to markets, inequality, and population growth, as the world population climbs toward an estimated 9.6 billion in 2050.

Roughly one-third of the food produced by farmers in low- and middle-income countries is lost between the field and the market. This loss may be due to pests, mold, or other factors that destroy the food. In high-income countries, a similar amount is wasted between the market and the table, according to the UN's Food and Agriculture Organization.

Food Insecurity in the United States

Statistics can trail behind reality. The numbers reported here were likely much higher in 2020 due to the COVID-19 pandemic and economic downturn. The nation's largest network of food banks reported a 70% increase in demand due to COVID-19. In April 2020, 44% of all Americans were afraid they would not be able to afford food.

According to the US Department of Agriculture (USDA), 37.2 million people lived in food-insecure households in the US in 2018. That's over 11% of the total US population. The rates are higher in households with children, especially those led by single mothers, 27.8% of which experience food insecurity.

Food insecurity is more common in large cities and rural areas. It is less common in suburban areas. According to Food Forward, "Food insecurity rates are highest in the South, where on average 12% of households experience food insecurity. The next highest are several states in the Midwest/Appalachian region: Kentucky, West Virginia, Ohio, and Indiana."

Race makes a difference: 8.1% of white households experience food insecurity, 21.2% of Black households experience food insecurity, and 16.2% of Hispanic households experience food insecurity. The data does not include other racial groups.

Age also makes a difference. Over 13% of Americans age 65 and over live in poverty. Most people age 65 and older receive the majority of their income from Social Security. Social Security is a government program that provides monthly payments to retired workers age 65 or older. The amount an individual receives is related to the amount of income they earned in their lifetime. Without Social Security, an additional 21.7 million Americans would be poor—47.5% of the senior population.

Between 11 percent and 38 percent of students enrolled in community colleges reported "very low" levels of food security in one study. Black, multiethnic, and Latinx students are more likely to report challenges with hunger. When college students go hungry or don't get proper nutrition, their grades suffer along with their physical and mental health.

Organizations to Contact

The editors have compiled the following list of organizations concerned with the issues debated in this book. The descriptions are derived from materials provided by the organizations. All have publications or information available for interested readers. The list was compiled on the date of publication of the present volume; the information provided here may change. Be aware that many organizations take several weeks or longer to respond to inquiries, so allow as much time as possible for the receipt of requested materials.

Barilla Center for Food & Nutrition Foundation (BCFN)
Via Madre Teresa di Calcutta, 3/a
Parma 43121
Italy
website: www.barillacfn.com/en/
contact form: https://www.barillacfn.com/en/contacts/
The BCFN Foundation addresses major food-related issues around the world. It works from "the environmental, economic and social perspective, to secure the wellbeing and health of people and the planet." On the website, learn about recent research and download publications.

Brighter Green
165 Court Street, #171
Brooklyn, NY 11201
(212) 414-2339, ext. 15
email: info@brightergreen.org
website: https://brightergreen.org/
Brighter Green is a public policy action tank. It works "to raise awareness of and encourage policy action on issues that span the environment, animals, and sustainability." The website offers articles, videos, podcasts, and additional resources.

Center on Budget and Policy Priorities
1275 First Street NE, Suite 1200
Washington, DC 20002
(202) 408-1080
email: center@cbpp.org
website: www.cbpp.org/
The Center on Budget and Policy Priorities is a progressive American think tank. Its website addresses research in various areas, including poverty and inequality, food assistance, and health.

Concern Worldwide US
355 Lexington Avenue, 16th Floor
New York, NY, 10017
(212) 557-8000
email: info.usa@concern.net
website: www.concernusa.org
This humanitarian organization specializes in emergency response, health and nutrition, and more for the world's most vulnerable people. The website describes its activities and impact and shares worldwide news.

Food Empowerment Project
PO Box 7322
Cotati, CA 94931
(707) 779-8004
email: info@foodispower.org
website: https://foodispower.org/
This volunteer-based nonprofit organization's mission statement is "to create a more just and sustainable world by recognizing the power of one's food choices." Learn about veganism, the rights of farmworkers, child labor, and access to food.

Food Forward
7412 Fulton Avenue, Suite #3
North Hollywood, CA 91605
(818) 764-1022
email: info@foodforward.org
website: foodforward.org/

Food Forward rescues thousands of pounds of surplus produce each week and donates it to hunger relief agencies across Southern California. The "Learn" tab on the website has stats about food security.

Population Connection
2120 L Street NW, Suite 500
Washington, DC 20037
(202) 332-2200
email: info@popconnect.org
website: www.populationconnection.org/
Population Connection is a nonprofit organization that raises awareness of challenges associated with family planning and the global population. Its Population Education program provides hands-on lesson plans.

World Health Organization (WHO)
Avenue Appia 20
1211 Geneva
website: www.who.int/
contact form: www.who.int/about/who-we-are/contact-us
WHO is an agency of the United Nations responsible for international public health. WHO's main goal is "the attainment by all peoples of the highest possible level of health."

The World Resources Institute
10 G Street NE, Suite 800
Washington, DC 20002
(202) 729-7600
website: www.wri.org/
This global research nonprofit organization is focused on seven areas: food, forests, water, energy, cities, climate and ocean. Learn about its food programs and reports from around the world.

For Further Reading

Books

Ashley, Jon Michael. *Food Security in the Developing World*. Amsterdam, Netherlands: Academic Press, 2016. This title covers the extent of food insecurity, its causes, and options for the future.

Fukuoka, Masanobu. *Sowing Seeds in the Desert: Natural Farming, Global Restoration, and Ultimate Food Security*. Hartford, VT: Chelsea Green Publishing, 2013. The author shares his plan to rehabilitate the deserts of the world using natural farming.

Hossfeld, Leslie, E. Brooke Kelly, and Julia Waity. *Food and Poverty: Food Insecurity and Food Sovereignty Among America's Poor*. Nashville, TN: Vanderbilt University Press, 2018. This title explores the forces at play in food production and distribution, and how that affects individuals' lifestyles.

Little, Amanda. *The Fate of Food: What We'll Eat in a Bigger, Hotter, Smarter World*. New York, NY: Harmony Books, 2019. A professor and journalist explores how we will feed 9 billion people sustainably in the coming decades.

Rowe, Martin. *Beyond the Impossible: The Futures of Plant-Based and Cellular Meat and Dairy*. New York, NY: Brighter Green 2019. The author imagines what the US might look like as a vegan country with plant-based meat substitutes. A free download is available at https://brightergreen.org/wp-content/uploads/2019/07/Beyond-the-Impossible.pdf.

Searchinger, Tim, Richard Waite, Craig Hanson, and Janet Ranganathan. *Creating a Sustainable Food Future: A Menu of Solutions to Feed Nearly 10 Billion People, by 2050*. Washington, DC: World Resources Institute, 2019. The report offers five solutions that can work together to help us feed the future without destroying the planet. A shorter version of the report is available online at https://wrr-food.wri.org/sites/default/files/2019-07/creating-sustainable-food-future_2_5.pdf.

Tickell, Josh. *Kiss the Ground: How the Food You Eat Can Reverse Climate Change, Heal Your Body & Ultimately Save Our World*. New York NY: Simon & Schuster, 2017. The author explains how we can change our diets to "reverse global warming, harvest healthy, abundant food, and eliminate the poisonous substances that are harming our children, pets, bodies, and ultimately our planet."

Wise, Timothy A. *Eating Tomorrow: Agribusiness, Family Farmers, and the Battle for the Future of Food.* New York, NY: The New Press, 2019. The author argues that small farms, rather than large agribusiness, are the way to grow more and healthier food.

Periodicals and Internet Sources

Bauer, Lauren, "The COVID-19 Crisis Has Already Left Too Many Children Hungry in America," the Brookings Institution, May 6, 2020. https://www.brookings.edu/blog/up-front/2020/05/06/the-covid-19-crisis-has-already-left-too-many-children-hungry-in-america/

Boston University Medical Center, "Lifting Children Out of Food Insecurity," October 13, 2016. https://www.disabled-world.com/fitness/nutrition/foodsecurity/security.php

Drexel University, "Social Stigma Can Stand in the Way of Food Insecurity Screening," March 23, 2018. https://www.disabled-world.com/fitness/nutrition/foodsecurity/snap-stigma.php

Faculty of Science, University of Copenhagen, "Six-Legged Livestock—Edible Insect Farming," May 15, 2017. https://www.disabled-world.com/fitness/nutrition/foodsecurity/crickets.php

Feeding America, "Millions of Eligible Seniors Not Receiving Federal Benefits," May 28, 2016. https://www.disabled-world.com/fitness/nutrition/foodsecurity/fed-benifits.php

Hart, Marion, and Sarah Ferguson, "What Is Ready-to-Use Therapeutic Food?" UNICEF, March 6, 2019. https://www.unicefusa.org/stories/what-ready-use-therapeutic-food/32481

IPBES, "Current World Land Degradation Affecting Health of Billions," October 10, 2018. https://www.disabled-world.com/fitness/nutrition/foodsecurity/land-degradation.php

Lendman, Stephen, "Millions Hungry and Food Insecure in the US," Global Research, October 16, 2019. https://www.globalresearch.ca/millions-hungry-food-insecure-us/5692168

Lund, Jay, Josue Medellin, John Durand, and Kathleen Stone, "Droughts and Progress—Lessons from California's 2012-2016 Drought," PreventionWeb, January 27, 2019. https://www.preventionweb.net/news/view/63341

Ohio State University, "American Consumers Throw Out 80 Billion Pounds of Food a Year," July 22, 2016. https://www.disabled-world.com/fitness/nutrition/foodsecurity/wasteful.php

Smith, Vincent H., "Global Markets Can Help Reduce Climate-Driven Food Insecurity," IFPRI Blog, December 18, 2019. https://www.ifpri.org/blog/global-markets-can-help-reduce-climate-driven-food-insecurity

University of Missouri, "Local Food Key to Improving Food Security," May 12, 2011. https://www.disabled-world.com/fitness/nutrition/foodsecurity/local-food.php

Washington University School of Medicine, "Stunted Growth Linked to Dietary Deficiencies," February 24, 2016. https://www.disabled-world.com/fitness/nutrition/foodsecurity/stunted.php

Websites

The Hope Center for College, Community, and Justice
(hope4college.com/)
The Hope Center at Temple University addresses college students' needs for food, affordable housing, transportation, and child care. The website describes its projects, research, and resources.

Our World in Data (ourworldindata.org)
Our World in Data focuses on research and tackling world problems such as poverty, hunger, climate change, and disease. Find publications on its website.

Youth in Motion for Climate Action!
(http://www.fao.org/3/ca5746en/CA5746EN.pdf)
A compilation of youth initiatives in agriculture to address the impacts of climate change, from the Food and Agriculture Organization of the United Nations.

Index

A
Abbassian, Abdolreza, 45
Ackerman, Jennifer, 82–88
Africa, 18, 42, 44, 45, 48, 58, 93, 103, 105, 106
AgriProtein, 106
Amos, Valerie, 42
Arria, Amelia M., 27
arthritis, 36

B
Bangladesh, 58
Benn, Hilary, 43
Beyer, Peter, 87, 88
Brazil, 104, 105
Brennhofer, Stephanie, 27
Brooks, Mo, 36
Broton, Katharine M., 24, 26
Bruening, Meg, 27

C
Caldeira, Kimberly M., 27
cancer, 36
Center on Budget and Policy Priorities, 29–34
China, 104, 105
chronic obstructive pulmonary disease (COPD), 36
climate change, and food security, 8, 20, 52, 55–60
Coca-Cola, 94
Concern Worldwide US, 55–60

D
DellaPenna, Dean, 87
Democratic Republic of Congo (DRC), 44, 52
Devereux, Stephen, 50
Devex, Michael Igoe, 89–96
diabetes, 8, 70–71
Dyson, Tim, 46

E
Egypt, 44
El Zein, Aseel, 26
Ethiopia, 42, 96

F
famine, and population growth, 48–53
Fedoroff, Nina V., 46
Fondazione Barilla Center for Food & Nutrition, 17–20
Food and Agricultural Organization of the United Nations (FAO), 18–19, 20, 43, 44–45, 57–58, 78, 79, 95, 103, 106
food deserts, 67–75
Food Empowerment Project, 67–75
Food Forward, 11–16
food production
  and land ownership, 8, 89–96
  and technology, 77–81

food security/insecurity
  and climate change, 8, 20, 52, 55–60
  and college students, 7, 21–28, 61–66
  explanation of, 12, 13, 18
  and food deserts, 67–75
  and hunger, difference between, 14
  and link to chronic diseases, 8, 35–39
  and population growth, 8, 41–46, 47–54, 78
  and seniors, 7, 18, 29–34
Freudenberg, Nicholas, 23

G
genetically modified foods, 9, 82–88
Ghana, 104, 105
Global Hunger Index (GHI), 51–52, 56
golden rice, 87–88
Goldrick-Rab, Sara, 23, 26
greenhouse gas emissions, 57, 60, 79, 99, 100, 103, 105, 106

H
Harris, Frank, III, 25
Hasell, Joe, 47–54
heart disease, 8, 36, 70, 71
Hellmich, Rick, 84
hepatitis, 36
high blood pressure/hypertension, 36, 38
Hunnes, Dana Ellis, 97–101
Hunter, Ashley, 77–81

I
India, 45, 85, 103
insects, eating, 9, 102–107

K
Keefe, Jack, 96
Kenya, 42, 103
kidney disease, 36
Kline, Nate, 90, 92, 95
Kula, Olaf, 91, 93, 94

L
Lake, Anthony, 42
Laska, Melissa, 27
LeBlanc, Rick, 102–107
Lesher, William G., 45–46
Liberia, 94
Linck, Henry, 28

M
Mai, Minhtuyen, 24
malnutrition/poor nutrition, 8, 18, 19, 36, 42, 45, 50, 57, 60, 85
Malthus, Thomas Robert, 48, 49, 50, 53
Maroto, Maya E., 28
Mexico, 45, 104
Moon, Emily, 61–66

N
Nestle, Marion, 87
Netherlands, 104

O
obesity, 8, 19, 70–71, 72
Ordway, Denise-Marie, 21–28

P

Papua New Guinea, 95
Patnaik, Biraj, 44
Payne-Sturges, Devon C., 27
PepsiCo, 94
Perry, Susan, 35–39
plant-based diets/food, 97–101
Poppendieck, Janet, 23
Population Connection, 41–46
Population Institute, 78, 80
Porritt, Sir Jonathan, 48
Potrykus, Ingo, 87
Prakash, Channapatna, 85, 86, 87

S

Snelling, Anastasia, 28
Snow, Allison, 83, 84, 85
Somalia, 42, 48, 50, 52
South Africa, 103, 106
Stamoulis, Kostas, 45
stroke, 36
stunted growth in children, 42, 44, 45, 51
Supplemental Nutritional Assistance Program (SNAP), 23–24, 30, 32–33

T

Thailand, 103, 104, 105
Tjaden, Allison, 27
Todd, Michael, 27

U

Ukraine, 45
US Department of Agriculture (USDA), 7, 14, 15, 18, 36, 37–38, 39, 45, 68, 85

V

van Woerden, Irene, 27
Vietnam, 58
Vincent, Kathryn B., 27

W

Weaver, Kari E., 24
Wood, J. Luke, 25
World Health Organization (WHO), 18, 87

Y

Ynsect, 106

Picture Credits

Cover Ringo Chiu/Shutterstock.com; p. 10 Stephanie Keith/Getty Images; p. 13 monkeybusinessimages/iStock/Getty Images Plus; p. 19 Paula Bronstein/Getty Images; p. 25 Bernd Wüstneck/Picture Alliance via Getty Images; p. 32 Matt Jonas/Digital First Media/Boulder Daily Camera via Getty Images; p. 37 leezsnow/E+/Getty Images; p. 40 Francisco Emilio Duran/iStock/Getty Images Plus; p. 43 ranplett/E+/Getty Images; p. 51 Prakash Singh/AFP via Getty Images; p. 57 John Moore/Getty Images; p. 63 Derek Davis/Portland Press Herald via Getty Images; p. 70 Michal Cizek/AFP via Getty Images; p. 76 Chris Hondros/Getty Images; p. 79 Manan Vatsyayana/AFP via Getty Images; p. 86 Longhua Liao/Moment/Getty Images; p. 92 Tony Karumba/AFP via Getty Images; p. 100 Gordon Chibroski/Portland Press Herald via Getty Images; p. 104 Hoang Dinh Nam/AFP via Getty Images.